D1741870

1 MONTH OF
FREE
READING

at
www.ForgottenBooks.com

By purchasing this book you are eligible for one month membership to ForgottenBooks.com, giving you unlimited access to our entire collection of over 1,000,000 titles via our web site and mobile apps.

To claim your free month visit:
www.forgottenbooks.com/free1336144

* Offer is valid for 45 days from date of purchase. Terms and conditions apply.

ISBN 978-0-365-05755-0
PIBN 11336144

This book is a reproduction of an important historical work. Forgotten Books uses
state-of-the-art technology to digitally reconstruct the work, preserving the original format
whilst repairing imperfections present in the aged copy. In rare cases, an imperfection in
the original, such as a blemish or missing page, may be replicated in our edition. We do,
however, repair the vast majority of imperfections successfully; any imperfections that
remain are intentionally left to preserve the state of such historical works.

Forgotten Books is a registered trademark of FB &c Ltd.
Copyright © 2018 FB &c Ltd.
FB &c Ltd, Dalton House, 60 Windsor Avenue, London, SW19 2RR.
Company number 08720141. Registered in England and Wales.

For support please visit www.forgottenbooks.com

Historic, Archive Document

Do not assume content reflects current
scientific knowledge, policies, or practices.

RED RADIANCE

THIS business was established by L. J. Farmer in
when he was a lad of 17 years. Strawberry plants
first grown and sold, but later on, all kinds of
plants; and finally shrubs, trees and everything that go
make up a complete nursery business. Most people lil
buy all their supplies at one place to save transport
charges, and we try to accommodate them.

Order Trees, Shrubs, Plants, Vines, Etc.,
Collect on Delivery

We understand that it is not always convenient fo
our patrons to send in the full remittance when they
their orders. Please do not put off ordering on accou
this. We recommend that you send in your order as
as possible with the understanding that the goods are
shipped C. O. D. for the full amount, less whatever
payment may have been made at time of ordering.
recommend that one-fourth of the full amount be sent
the order, if possible, as a guarantee of good faith. No
will be booked and held for a customer, unless some pay
is made at time of ordering. We will accept personal cl
or any established method of remitting money.

ransportation Costs; a Gift with Every Order

$2.00 or more will receive their choice of a packet of Cape Goos
gold seeds. If your order comes to $10.00 or more, we send you a co
catalog, but a treatise on strawberry culture (112 pages, 44 illustrat
r more, you receive a beautiful framed dining-room picture, show
vith bananas by the side. The picture, if purchased alone, would c
help pay parcel post or express charges, we give you choice bulb
your order. If your order amounts to $10.00, you get 10 times as
order amounted to but $1.00, but every customer gets something
d last year with the Dahlias and Gladioli we gave them. This yea
a surplus of many valuable things which we propose to give away
understood, however, that no attention will be paid to requests for s
s of which we have a surplus.

Our Regular Shipping Season

or spring begins in March and lasts until some time in June. Ou
until December, or until the ground freezes solid. We ship special
n the year.

the year. There is hardly a week, winter or su
n made as low as | that we do not make shipments somewhere. Our
good stock. We | cipal business is in the United States, mainly ir
ding slogan, but | York and adjoining states, but we have succe
the best goods at | shipped to Central and South America, Europe,
r customers from | New Zealand, Australia and South Africa. M
every transaction | our orders come by mail, but the business of s
yer as well as to | ing home and near-by-customers, who come b
Post, Express or | and truck, is increasing each year. Utica and
mount to at least | are to our east. Rochester and Oswego to ou
Watertown and Ogdensburg to the north, while

?lease | cuse and Binghamton are to the south of us.
round trip from any of these cities to our pla
our line, at any | be easily made in a day and hundreds make the
lmost all times of | to purchase goods of us each year.

IMPORTANT

packing all orders so that they reach the customer in good condition.
e in satisfactory condition, due to delay in transit or other cau
at we may take steps for immediate adjustment. We stand ready
ll complaints must be filed within five days after receipt of the shi
ications to L. J. Farmer, Pulaski, N. Y.

t to us.

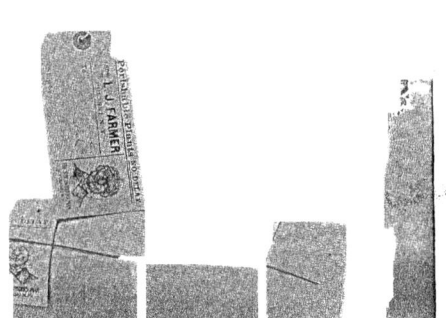

es of shipping packages most commonly used by us, the bundle and
)0 plants are usually packed in bundles, reinforced with cardboard to
Orders of 250 to 500 plants or more are packed in market baskets.
thousand plants, are packed in crates or boxes. Small orders of trees
: orders of 100 or more trees are usually shipped in long boxes.

ιtrawberries

∶rries 12 to 18 inches apart in the row, with rows 2 to 3 feet
he same distance in the row, but make the rows 4 to 5 feet
∙e feet in an acre and you can find the number of plants that
by the multiplied distance between the plants. Thus an acre
3,712 plants and an acre set 4 x 1 contains a little over 10,000
to find the number of plants or trees of any kind that can be
e to set strawberries in the North is early spring, but trans-
∶ in the growing season and pot grown plants are best set in
tober and November are best months for setting strawberry
ates.

,ASSIFIED   er, Klondike, Gandy, Lupton, Mascot, The Best, Early
  Early Jersey   Jersey Giant.
ooper, Sharp-

DESCRIPTIONS, PRICES, ETC.

lasting, Come

Varieties marked "P." are perfect in flower and will
bear well when planted alone. Varieties marked
:us, Marshall,   "Imp." are imperfect in flower and need to be planted
i, Chesapeake,   near some perfect flowered variety that blossoms at
the same time.

Early Ozark,   We have tried to make our descriptions plain and
  Brandywine,   not misleading. It is sometimes difficult for the be-
ginner to make the proper selection, however, and we

SOME SPECIMENS OF JUMBO STRAWBERRY GREATLY REDUCED

Strawberries

DESCRIPTION OF VARIETIES

EXTRA EARLY VARIETIES

Premier (P.)—Berry very large, oblong, light scarlet, attractive. Plants moderate growers, enormously productive. Very popular, doing best on light to medium light soils. Has produced at the rate of 16,000 qts. to the acre in this section. See illustration on back cover. 10 plants 50c; 25, 75c; 100, $1.50; 1000, $10.00.

Howard No. 17—Same variety as Premier.

Early Ozark—Berries large, firm, dark, rich colored, fine for shipping or canning. Ripens very early, holds size. Plants rugged, healthy, very productive. Same price as Premier.

Campbell's Early (P.) — Berries medium to large, round, good color, firm, attractive. Plants good growers, very productive. Very hardy plants. Same price as Premier.

EARLY OZARK

Horsey (P.)—Fine for shipping and canning. Distinct, attractive, glossy appearance. Price same as Premier.

Missionary (P.)—The long pointed berry we see in large city markets in February. Adapted for Florida, California, etc. Plants vigorous. Berries glossy, attractive. Price same as Premier.

Klondike (P.)—The favorite on the South Atlantic coast from Maryland down. Plants vigorous, with reddish cast. Berries medium size, firm, light colored, good shippers. Price same as Premier.

Early Jersey Giant (P.)—This berry has the color, large size, flavor and glossiness of the Marshall; combined with the productiveness of Premier. The plants are good growers. We have picked them as they run, twenty to the quart. 10 plants 65c; 25, $1.00; 100, $2.50; 1000, $20.00.

MEDIUM EARLY VARIETIES

Senator Dunlap (P.)—The universal favorite, sometimes called the lazy man's berry, because it will grow and produce with so little care. Plants extremely vigorous, making many runners; healthy. Berries medium in size, deep red, fine flavor, good for canning. Most largely grown of any variety by farmers and amateurs. 10 plants 35c; 25, 60c; 100, $1.25; 1000, $8.00; 10,000, $75.00.

Warfield (Imp.)—Similar to Dunlap in growth of vine and appearance of fruit. Enormously productive, medium size, rich dark red, good canner and shipper. 10 plants 50c; 25, 75c; 100, $1.50; 1000, $10.00.

Haverland (Imp.)—Plants healthy, vigorous and enormously productive, the berries laying about the plants literally in heaps and piles. Fruit oblong, light colored, glossy, with small hull. Same price as Warfield.

4

Strawberries

healthy and productive. Ber-
n and fine for market or home
red, but larger. Known under
ce same as Warfield.

hy, moderate growers, making
colored, not very firm, but take
oductive.   10 plants 65c; 25,

erry that it bobs up every little
o, Corsican, Hundred Dollar,
ers are the same.   The plants
ndividual plants, very produc-
p glossy red on the sunny side
Price same as Warfield.

ng medium early strawberries.
very best of care to produce
1 6 berries that filled a quart
the very finest flavor.   The
.   Price same as Bubach.

same as Marshall. Same price.

it. Berries large, light colored,
eld.

healthy on well drained soils.
and attractive.   Price same as

NEW YORK OR OSWEGO, ETC.

variety intro-
e, healthy and
we grow.   Ber-
d shippers, sell-

ing sometimes at $1.00 per quart in the New York
market.   It is so enormously productive that it does
not seem to have time to bear all its fruit in the
regular season, and often bears quite a crop in the
late fall on the same plants that have borne the large
spring crop, although it is not an everbearing sort,
so called.   They were especially fruitful the past fall,
producing such a quantity that many crates were
shipped from this locality to the New York market
in October.   Prices: 10 plants 75c; 25, $1.25; 100,
$3.50; 1000, $25.00.

Sharpless (P.)—Fine growing plants, moderately

Strawberries

Chesapeake (P.)—Plants good growers, but require th care. They sell at 35 to 40c per quart wholesale, year ε in the New York market, when some kinds go begging. to late varieties, what Marshall is to early ones. The patient grower will be well rewarded by growing Chesapea ries large, very firm, with golden seeds and of the very fin Prices: 10 plants 65c; 25, $1.00; 100, $2.50; 1000, $20.0

Stevens' Late Champion (P.)—Plants vigorous runner: and do well everywhere. Berries large, light colored, good shippers. One of the best and most profitable for to distant markets. Price same as Sharpless.

Mascot (P.)—Plants ideal growers, enormously prod deep, dark red, fine flavored berries. Ripens very late, a latest of all. Price same as Chesapeake.

The Best (P.)—We introduced and named this "The cause it is the best all around berry we have ever grow and year out. The only complaint we ever had for it is not over productive in some years. Plants strong, sturd with heavy, leathery foliage, free of disease. Berries lig glossy, attractive, round, as if turned in a lathe, with dim denture in the tip end. One of the latest of all strawbe plants 60c; 25, $1.00; 100, $3.00; 1000, $25.00.

Big Late (Imp.)—A favorite for market parts. Large plants, very productive of v fruits, attractive and fine in every way. P as Sharpless.

IG

:, vigorous plants. Ber- light colored and pro- : favorite in Missouri everywhere. It seems wberry as the Dunlap the best looking straw- rom the South the past is.

Sharpless.

Sharpless.

:, healthy plants, pro- ery large, dark glossy ame as Sharpless.

ze, vigorous, tall grow- Berries smooth, glossy, ·ere most favorably im- .st season. Price same

STEVENS' LATE CHAMPION STRAWBE

BEGINNERS' STRAWBERRY COLLECTI

| 25 Premier | 25 Sen. Dunlap |
| 25 Mastodon Everbearing | 25 Warfield |

Catalog Price, $3.35—Collection Price, $2.2

BEGINNERS' STRAWBERRY COLLECTI
FOR MARKET

250 Premier	250 Glen Mary
250 New York	250 Mastodon
250 Sen. Dunlap	100 Champion Everbeari

Special Collection Price, $19.00

EVERBEARING STRAWBERRY COLLEC]

| 25 Mastodon | 25 Superb |
| 25 Americus | 25 Champion Everbe |

Catalog Price, $5.00—Collection Price, $4.(
OR

500 Mastodon	100 Americus
200 Champion Everbearing	25 Come Back
100 Everlasting	100 Superb

Collection Price, $28.00

:RY

6

MASTODON
EVERBEARING
STRAWBERRY

Everbearing Strawberries

WE were the first nurserymen and strawberry growers to realize the great possibilities and merits of the fall or Everbearing strawberries. Many of the leading strawberry nurserymen, who are pushing them strongly, thought they were but a fleeting, passing novelty. Today, there is nothing quite so popular in the Horticultural world as Everbearing strawberries and many growers have made a lot of money out of them for fruit. We have no fruit or other growing crop on our farm that pays us better than these strawberries for the fruit alone.

Mastodon (P.)—This is the latest wonder in the everbearing line. It originated near Peru, Indiana, by George W. Voer, a veteran strawberry grower, who crossed Kellogg's Prize with Superb. Like many an originator of new fruits, it is said that Mr. Voer got very little for this new strawberry; unscrupulous parties practically stealing it away from him. In fact, this is what he told me.

On our grounds, the soil being a stony upland, the Mastodon surpasses all other kinds of everbearing strawberries. We notice in heavy clay spots that the fruit is larger and more abundant. On the lighter soils, it is not so productive and the berries are not of as good color, but are large and otherwise just the same. We have fruited it for four years. It averages larger than any summer bearing strawberry we ever had in fruit. The berries were very large and uniform the forepart of the season, but in the height of the season there were many inferior berries due to something that interfered with proper pollenization. Later in the season the fruits were almost perfect. We sold most of our berries to a truckman, who paid us 30c per quart at the door. Many were sold to tourists and local people, and for these we received 35c per quart. From the two acres of Mastodon, we received over $1000.00. We paid 5c per quart for picking and our men, who were paid $3.00 to $3.50 per day, would sometimes earn more than their daily wages. The heaviest picking was one day in October, when

late August, estimated that we would pick 300 bushels of berries from the two acres, but the cold, unfavorable weather reduced the crop to a little less than half of this. When the ground froze solid about December 1st, there were crates and crates of berries large enough, but lacking color and flavor at this time of the year. The above appeared in our 1928 catalog. We have no cause to change our opinion of the Mastodon strawberry after another year's experience. The fall of 1928 was even more unfavorable than the year before and the results were not as satisfactory as in 1927, but Mastodon is still the very best everbearing strawberry with us. In favorable years, we have had more satisfactory crops of Champion than we have had of Mastodon during the past few years and we wonder what Mastodon would do under favorable weather conditions. It certainly would surprise people. One thing not generally mentioned about the Mastodon, is that it is such a fine berry in the early summer season, the largest and best keeper, as well as the most productive of them all. The Mastodon is now the most popular one variety of strawberry in America. 10 plants 75c; 25, $1.25; 100, $4.00; 1000, $25.00.

Champion Everbearing (P)—10 plants 65c; 25, $1.00; 100, $2.50; 1000, $20.00.

Americus (P)—The best flavored strawberry in cultivation. 10 plants $1.00; 25, $1.50; 100, $5.00.

Come Back (P.)—10 plants $1.00; 25, $1.50; 100,

PORTLAND GRAPE
(See Description, Page 15)

CUTHBERT RED RASPBERRIES
(See Description, Page 10)

PERFECTION CURRANT
(See Description, Page 14)

ELDORADO BLACKBERRY
(See Description, Page 13)

ws young plant just potted.   Figure 7 shows small bunch of transplanted plants.
ws young runner plant in August.   Figure 8 shows transplanted plant, earth clinging to roots.
        Figure 9 shows plant in pot.

Transplanted Strawberry Plants
(Strawberry Plants for Summer Planting)

on the same general plan as transplanted vegetable plants, etc. We prepare
ollows. In early spring we take ordinary layer plants and trench them in little
t 1 inch apart in the row, with rows 6 to 8 inches apart. These plants start slowly,
root growth but not much top growth. When they are taken up for shipment or
ng to our own fields, any time after May 1st, it is found that the roots have sent
fibrous rootlets which retain the soil, preventing it from all dropping off. At the
tops have grown but little and we find that such plants survive the final trans-
better than plants taken from the fruiting fields that are not transplanted. These
have recovered from the "Shock"that strawberry plants usually get when trans-
nstead of wilting down and taking much time to recover, they start at once and
ng, making as good a growth of plants and new runners as ordinary plants do
t least a month or six weeks earlier. Our book, "Farmer on the Strawberry," ex-
re fully. Price, 50c.

PRICES OF TRANSPLANTED PLANTS
Ready in May, June, July and August

zark, Campbell's Early, Warfield, Haverland, Parson's Beauty, New York, Sharpless, Glen
:, Brandywine, Sample, Nick Ohmer, Aroma, Gandy, Big Joe, Kellogg's Prize, Lupton, Big
npion. 10 plants 50c; 25, 75c; 100, $2.50; 1000, $20.00.
.nlap—10 plants 40c; 25, 65c; 100, $2.00; 1000, $17.00.
' Giant, Bubach, Marshall, Norwood, Cooper, Mascot, The Best, Progressive, Champion Ever-
Chesapeake. 10 plants 65c; 25, $1.00; 100, $3.00; 1000, $25.00.
stodon, Americus, Everlasting, Come Back. 10 plants $1.00; 25, $1.50; 100, $5.00; 1000,

Pot Grown Strawberries
r Spring, Summer and Fall of 1929. Orders for 100 plants may call for 4 kinds

	Dozen	100	1000		Dozen	100	1000
....	$1.00	$6.00	$50.00	Nick Ohmer	$1.00	$6.00	$50.00
....	1.00	6.00	50.00	Norwood	1.00	7.00	60.00
....	1.00	6.00	50.00	Ozark	1.00	6.00	50.00
....	1.00	6.00	50.00	Parson's Beauty	1.00	6.00	50.00
....	1.00	7.00	60.00	Premier	1.00	6.00	50.00
....	1.00	6.00	50.00	Sample	1.00	6.00	50.00
....	1.00	7.00	60.00	Senator Dunlap	1.00	6.00	45.00
....	1.00	7.00	60.00	Sharpless	1.00	6.00	50.00
....	1.00	7.00	60.00	S. L. Champion	1.00	6.00	50.00
....	1.00	6.00	50.00	Success	1.00	6.00	50.00
....	1.00	6.00	50.00	The Best	1.00	7.00	60.00
....	1.00	6.00	50.00'	Warfield	1.00	6.00	50.00
....	1.00	7.00	60.00	Wm. Belt	1.00	6.00	50.00
....	1.50	8.00	75.00		EVERBEARING		
....	1.00	6.00	50.00	Americus	$1.50	$10.00	
....	1.00	7.00	60.00	Champion Everbearing	1.25	8.00	$75.00
....	1.00	7.00	60.00	Everlasting	1.50	10.00	85.00
....	1.00	6.00	50.00	Mastodon	1.50	10.00	85.00
....	1.00	6.00	50.00	Progressive	1.25	8.00	75.00
....	1.00	6.00	50.00	Superb	1.25	8.00	75.00

A NICE BASKET OF REDPATH RASPBERRIES. PHOTO SEPTEMBER 16TH

Raspberries

FOR garden culture raspberries can be set quite close if necesary, but the bush grows larger and is more fruitful if the plants are given sufficient room for full development. Red raspberries are usually set 1 to 3 feet apart in the row, with rows 5 to 6 feet apart. If they are set 3 x 6, it takes about 2400 to the acre or 15 to the square rod. Black raspberries are usually set the same distance in the rows as the red varieties, but the rows are made about 7 feet apart. Purple raspberries are often set even farther apart than black raspberries. Thus it usually takes a few more than 2000 plants to set an acre of blackcaps and a few less than 2000 to set an acre of purple raspberries. Raspberry plants do best when set in a dormant condition in the early spring or late fall, but can be set any time with success if care is taken in planting. Plant only raspberry plants that are free of the disease called Mosaic. The plants we have to offer have been inspected according to the rules of the State of New York and are free of diseases.

Redpath (Latham)—Originated in the hardy climate of Minnesota where it is practically taking the place of all other varieties of red raspberries. Redpath is a natural selection from the Latham, being more immune to the ravages of Mosaic, more vigorous and productive, larger and finer every way. The canes are hardy and enormously productive, having the characteristic of bearing a satisfactory crop in the fall of the same year that the plants are set. The berries are large, of good color, firm, and ripen later than most varieties, thus prolonging the season. We believe it the most profitable red raspberry now before the public. Prices: 15c each; 10 plants, $1.00; 25, $1.75; 100, $5.00; 1000, $35.00. Transplants: 20c each; 10 plants $1.50; 25, $2.50; 100, $7.50; 1000, $60.00. Small plants, with small tops, but well rooted, 10c each; 10 plants, 75c; 25, $1.25; 100, $3.50; 1000, $25.00.

Saint Regis—This is the earliest red raspberry that we grow. The canes are very hardy and vigorous. Berries bright red in color, medium in size, good flavored and very attractive in the basket. It is the most satisfactory fall fruiting raspberry we have on our grounds. Prices: 10c each; 10 plants, 50c; 25, $1.00; 100, $3.00; 1000, $25.00. Transplants: 15c each; 10 plants, 75c; 25, $1.50; 100, $5.00; 1000, $40.00.

Cuthbert—The old standby. Vigorous and very productive. Berries large, oblong, deep rich red, of highest quality. Prices same as Saint Regis.

Herbert—Canes moderate growers, very hardy and productive. Berries large, oval in shape, of good quality and of fine appearance. Does not incumber the ground with useless canes like some varieties. Least subject to disease of any variety. Requires rich soil and good care to do its best. Originated in Canada and is a great favorite in private gardens and where quality is appreciated. Price same as Redpath.

10

ST. REGIS EVERBEARING RASPBERRY

Raspberries

Hardy, very productive, large fruit. Fine
ng, being quite acid. Price same as Red-

une—Hardy, smooth canes. Most produc-
early red raspberry. Fruit soft but fine fla-
rice same as Redpath.

Queen—Canes very similar to Cuthbert, of
is probably a sport. Berries golden-yellow
fine flavored. It seems to be even better
than Cuthbert and can be grown and mixed
er varieties in canning to enhance the fine
Price same as Redpath.

Red Raspberry (New) — Originated in
it Ontario Exp. Sta. A cross of Herbert and
. Canes taller and heavier than Cuthbert
ot break with the heavy crop of fruit, almost
rickers. Fruit larger than Cuthbert, firm and
ell. Color resembles Marlboro, being bright,
. Ripens early and brings highest prices in
Highly recommended by the best Canadian
s. Strong transplants, 25c each; 10 plants,
, $3.50; 100, $15.00; 1000, $100.00.
—A Super-Cuthbert. Price same as Red-

-A hardy, vigorous variety, very productive.
il, of the Cuthbert type, not quite so large
but more firm. Price same as Redpath.

nce and Erskine Park—Price same as Red-

PLATE OF HERBERT RASPBERRIES

DARK RED RASPBERRIES

Columbian (See back cover)—The universal favorite, succeeds wherever any kind of raspberry will
grow. Canes are mammoth, often an inch or more
in diameter. Enormously productive of very large,
dark colored or purple berries of fair quality. When
canned or preserved, they are unsurpassed. It is
probably a cross between the red and black raspberry.
It does not send up suckers to encumber the ground
like weeds, but makes new plants from the tip ends of
the canes, like black caps. Prices of tip plants; 10c
each; 10 plants, 75c; 25, $1.25; 100, $4.00; 1000,
$25.00. Strong transplants: 20c each; 10 plants,
$1.50; 25, $2.00; 100, $6.00; 1000, $50.00.

ROYAL
PURPLE
RASPBERRY

Royal Purple—Similar to Columbian, entirely hardy
at all times and on all soils. Canes are smooth. Berries are large, dark red, good flavor, especially when
canned. For heavy soils and extremely cold locations,
it is great. We have a fine supply on hand. Tips: 15c
each; 10 plants, $1.00; 25, $2.00; 100, $6.00; 1000,
$50.00. Transplants: 25c each; 10 plants, $1.75; 25,
$3.50; 100, $12.00.

FAMILY RASPBERRY COLLECTION

25 Columbian	25 Cuthbert
25 Golden Queen	25 Plum Farmer

Catalog Price, $5.00—Collection Price, $4.00
Price of Above in Transplanted Plants
Catalog Price, $8.00—Collection Price, $7.00

11

TYPICAL FRUITING BRANCHES OF PLUM FARMER BLACK RASPBERRY

Black Raspberries

Plum Farmer—The most popular black raspberry now before the public. Introduced by us over twenty-five years ago. Now grown almost exclusively from the Atlantic to the Pacific. Canes clean, healthy growers, vigorous and free from disease. The berries are very large, thick meated, with few seeds. It ripens real early, producing its crop in a bunch, thus making room for other varieties. When the leaves drop in the fall, the canes are of a beautiful silvery-blue color. The fruit is grayish-black. Prices of tips: 10c each; 10 plants 60c; 25, $1.00; 100, $3.00; 1000, $25.00. Transplants: 15c each; 10 plants $1.00; 25, $2.00; 100, $7.50; 1000, $60.00.

Cumberland — A jet-black berry of good quality. Canes hardy, healthy and very productive. Largely grown in Pennsylvania and the West. Price same as Plum Farmer.

Winfield and Gregg—Price same as Plum Farmer.

Honey Sweet—As its name implies, very rich, sweet and of fine flavor. Canes hardy and productive. 15c each, 10 plants, 75c; 25, $1.50; 100, $5.00; 1000, $40.00. Transplants: 20c each; 10 plants $1.25; 25, $2.00; 100, $7.00; 1000, $60.00.

New Giant—Originated in Western New York. The bushes are giants, the canes growing larger and taller than any other black raspberry. The fruit is also larger and finer than any other well known raspberry. Price same as Honey Sweet.

PUTNAM COUNTY, NEW YORK

November 8th, 1928
The currant bushes, dewberries and raspberry plants were received in splendid shape.

MRS. J. K. LIVINGSTON.

CREEK COUNTY, OKLAHOMA

May 3rd, 1928
The recent order of raspberries, rhubarb, roses, etc., was all received in fine shape and we are so well pleased, we have decided to order of you the following,—

F. E. ELDRED.

THE "HONEY SWEET" BLACKCAP

12

ɪberries

receive
future,
1 slash-
rapidly
ɪre and
ɔuld be
ʹs made
ɔetween
nd well
ɛ paths,
ɪ season
ɪr fruit-
e.

. Canes
medium
canning
e berries
rs in this
d Snyder
ɪnts 65c;
l5c each;
00.

ce.
ve.
est.

uc-
ike

ler.
the

dy.
50;

ELDORADO BLACKBERRY

Albro—Transplants: 35c each; 10 plants $2.50; 25,
$5.00; 100, $15.00.

Un-named Blackberry Plants—We have 50,000 to
100,000 plants of good varieties of blackberries,
adapted for general cultivation, from which we have
lost the labels. We offer them at a bargain. They
will be well dug, well rooted plants. Prices: 10 plants
50c; 25, 75c; 100, $2.00; 1000, $18.00.

Logan Berry—15c each; 10 plants $1.25; 25, $2.00;
100, $7.50; 1000, $60.00. Transplants: 25c each; 10
plants $2.00; 25, $4.00; 100, $15.00.

Himalaya Berry—Price same as Logan Berry.

ʹetia Dewberry—The dewberry sprawls on the ground each
ike other vines, and must be taken up and tied to stakes or
each spring before fruiting. The canes are cut away after
g to make room to tie the new sets of canes the next spring.
ɪre hardy and very fruitful if well cared for. The berries
ɪck and resemble blackberries in shape and general appear-
ɔut ripen much earlier, about the same time as early rasp-
. They are not as rich in flavor as blackberries, but sell
on account of large size, appearance and earliness. The
tion must all be done early in the season before the canes
ɔer the ground. We think nothing in the small fruit line
greater possibilities than dewberry culture. Prices of plants:
ɪch; 10 plants 65c; 25, $1.25; 100, $3.00; 1000, $25.00.
ɔlants: 15c each, 10 plants $1.00; 25, $1.75; 100, $5.00;
$40.00.

FAMILY BLACKBERRY COLLECTION

25 Snyder   25 Rathburn
25 Eldorado   25 Lucretia Dewberry

Catalog Price, $5.00—Collection Price, $4.00

Transplanted Plants

Catalog Price, $7.25—Collection Price, $5.25

13

Currants and G

TO do their best, the currant and gooseberry require a very rich soil with a tenacious subsoil. The plants should be set in rows 5 to 7 feet apart, 3 feet apart in the row. When the bush gets crowded it is better to remove part of the old branches than to trim back the tips of all the branches. Best results are obtained by keeping up cultivation, early and late, except during the picking season. Worms are very destructive to currants and gooseberries, unless destroyed by some poison, such as Hellebore, Paris Green or Arsenate of Lead. We can now ship currant and gooseberry plants into any State in the Union, except a few isolated towns and counties which are given over almost exclusively to the culture of Pine Trees.

Currants

Wilder Currant—Probably more widely grown than any other variety. Highly recommended by the great currant authority, the late S. D. Willard. Bush, hardy and vigorous, very productive of large, bright red berries. Prices: 2-year plants 20c each; $1.50 per 10; $10.00 per 100.

Fay's Prolific—Enormously productive of very large fruit. Inclined to do better on light soils than other varieties. Price same as Wilder.

White Grape Currant—The best white variety. Fine for fresh table use, being sweeter and more delicious than other currants. Price same as Wilder.

Victoria Currant—Strong growing bush, very productive of deep red, large fruit. Price same as Wilder.

Red Cross Currant—Price same as Wilder.

Perfection Currant—A comparatively new variety of great merit, a seedling from a cross of the Fay and White Grape, resembling both in many respects. It has won medals and diplomas wherever displayed. We have fruited it for several years and consider it the best variety now before the public. Prices: 2-year, 30c each; $2.50 per 10; $20.00 per 100.

Diploma Currant—Another fine currant originated by the late Jacob Moore. It is considered superior to all others by many prominent growers. Plants healthy and very productive; fruit large, attractive and easily picked. Price, same as Perfection.

POORMAN GOOSEBERRY

Ass
dred f
labels.
Large
each;

F.

C

Th
ment
the b
on th
letter:
qualit
is hi{
nume
plant
The f
The (
$4.00
Th

14

ed upon for the first early berries of summer.

ries

iversal favorite for home
produce an almost in-
erries are medium sized,
s: 2-year, 25c each; $2.00

y popular white variety.
uctive of pale green fruits
. The standard white for
er 10; $20.00 per 100.
rry—A very large fruited
fruit is dull red, smooth,
Houghton. Price same

)rman.

seberry Plants—We have
varieties, 3 to 5 years old,
il to prices for 2-year-old

SEBERRY
ION

!ed Jacket
Ioughton
lection Price, $1.65

hes, 3-5-years old
:e, $2.25

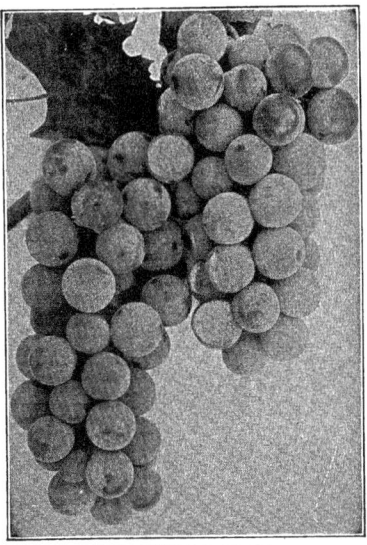

THE HUBBARD GRAPE

GRAPES

sunny location, it is preferable to plant on the south side of build-
i. A grapevine is as useful as any other vine in screening out un-
irlier and hardy varieties will ripen in most any location. Grapes
at is rich, mellow and well drained. Plant the vines from 6 to 10

PRUNING

ne should bear in mind that the fruit is borne on new wood which
ir's wood. When the vines are set, they should be cut back to with-
ie root. Every year, in November or early in the spring before the
be pruned freely. The object in pruning should be to get rid of
hout sacrificing too much of the new. In doing this, the old cane is
ies originate as near the ground as possible. The new canes that are
st one-third of their length. This allows plenty of space for the
fruit is produced. Several systems of pruning have been worked

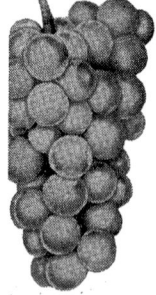

GRAPES

Hubbard—Quality fine, having that sweet and delicious flavor approaching the European varieties. ? Seeds few and small, separating easily from the tender pulp. Skin thin and firm. Berries and bunch large and uniform in shape. Ripens about 10 days ahead of Concord. Having finer quality, larger size, healthier foliage, and earlier fruiting season than the Concord or Niagara, and being as good a shipper and as strong a grower, the Hubbard is a much more desirable grape than either of these varieties. Price: 50c each.

Delaware—Red fruit, excellent flavor. 35c each.

Worden—Blue-black grape with thin skin; fine flavor. Price: 30c each.

Concord—The grape for the millions. Berries jet black. Price: 25c each.

Niagara—The most popular white grape. 30c each.

Lucile—This red grape ripens between Moore's Early and Worden, an excellent trio of our colors, red, white and blue. A good market grape in the North on account of productiveness and hardiness. Price: 35c each.

NIAGARA GRAPE

reen Mountain—Fruit yellowish-white. About the . reliable and earliest of well known varieties for North country. Price: 65c each.

ntario—Another new white grape which origi- d at the New York State Experiment Station at va. It is a seedling of Diamond crossed with n Mountain. Vine a good grower, productive. pens early, about with Green Mountain. It is of rior quality and especially recommended for home Price: 75c each.

itawba—The great wine grape. Still delicious all the other kinds are gone. Price: 30c each.

ssorted Grape Vines—We have several hundred e vines, all of them our very best varieties from h the labels have been lost. There appears to be varieties, all No. 1, 3-year vines. We will sell for 25c each; 5 vines for $1.00. 5 kinds if ed, but not labeled.

CHOICE GRAPE COLLECTION

Four 2-year Vines, the newest and finest varieties

1 Portland, white	1 Hubbard, black
1 Caco, wine-red	1 Lucile, red

Catalog Price, $2.35—Collection Price, $2.10

FARMER'S FAVORITE COLLECTION

Six No. 1, 2-year Vines for $1.50

1 Worden, blue	1 Moore's Early, black
1 Lucile, red	1 Diamond, white
1 Niagara, white	1 Concord, black

Catalog Price, $1.80—Collection Price, $1.50

GENERAL LIST OF GRAPE VINES

Prices given are for No. 1, 2-year-old-vines. 1-year vines will be supplied at two-thirds e prices and 3-year vines at 50% or one-half additional to the prices of 2-year-old vines. instance, 2-year-old Concords are 25c each. 1-year-olds will, therefore, cost 16 2-3 cents and ar-olds 37½ cents each. Prices given are for A No. 1 stock.

BLACK GRAPES

	Each	Per 10	Per 100
st Giant	$ .40	$3.50	$27.00
tus	.35	3.00	23.00
	.40	3.50	27.00
	.30	2.50	20.00
bell's Early	.40	3.50	27.00
ipion	.35	3.00	17.00
on	.35	3.00	17.00
ord	.25	2.00	15.00
ge	.35	3.00	23.00
Daisy	.40	3.50	27.00
Ohio	.60	4.50	40.00
Victor	.35	3.00	20.00
t	.35	3.00	27.00
ord	.35	3.00	20.00
ert	.35	3.00	23.00
ard	.50	4.00	35.00
lla	.35	3.00	20.00
	.35	3.00	17.00
ville	.35	3.00	20.00
imac	.50	4.00	35.00
e's Early	.30	2.50	20.00
	.50	4.00	35.00
on's	.50	4.00	35.00
raph	.35	3.00	23.00
er	.35	3.00	28.00
len	.30	2.50	20.00

RED GRAPES

	Each	Per 10	Per 100
am	$ .30	$2.50	$17.00
er Queen	.40	3.50	27.00
iton	.30	2.75	26.00
ant	.40	3.50	27.00
	.75	6.00	50.00
vba	.30	2.50	17.00
ipagne	.60	5.00	45.00
vare	.35	3.00	27.00

RED GRAPES—Continued

	Each	Per 10	Per 100
Diana	$ .35	$3.00	$20.00
Dracut Amber	.35	3.00	23.00
Dunkirk	1.00	9.00	
Gaertner	.35	3.00	27.00
Goethe	.35	3.00	27.00
Iona	.40	3.50	27.00
Jefferson	.60	5.00	45.00
Lindley	.30	2.50	17.00
Lucile	.35	3.00	20.00
Lutie	.35	3.00	20.00
Massasoit	.35	3.00	23.00
Moyer	.35	3.00	23.00
Perkins	.35	3.00	23.00
Regal	.40	3.50	30.00
Salem	.35	3.00	20.00
Urbana	1.25	3.00	20.00
Vergennes	.35	3.00	20.00
Woodruff Red	.35	3.00	28.00
Wyoming Red	.35	3.00	23.00

WHITE GRAPES

	Each	Per 10	Per 100
Brocton	$1.00		
Diamond	.30	$2.50	$20.00
Duchess	.30	2.50	23.00
Elvira	.35	3.00	27.00
Etta	.35	3.00	27.00
Green Mountain	.65	5.50	45.00
Hayes	.50	4.50	40.00
Jessica	.35	3.00	23.00
Martha	.35	3.00	23.00
Missouri Reissling	.35	3.00	20.00
Niagara	.30	2.50	18.00
Ontario	.75		
Pocklington	.30	2.75	26.00
Portland	.75	7.00	60.00
Rommel	.35	3.00	27.00

16

Farmer's Fruit Trees

NEW APPLES OF SPECIAL MERIT

Oswego—A distinct improvement over the Northern Spy, originated in Oswego County, New York, and introduced by us several years ago. Distinguished by its delightful flavor which equals its parent, the Northern Spy, and also by its clear, deep red color, even more attractive than the McIntosh. The typical fruit is as large or larger than the Northern Spy, but is more conical in shape. The flesh is firmer, making it a better keeper. We have kept specimens of the fruit until mid-summer in perfect condition. The young trees are vigorous growers and never show any signs of winter injury. It is an early and persistent bearer, and very productive. We recommend the Oswego as the best winter apple. Prices: 2 and 3 yr. trees, 5-7 ft., $1.25 each; $11.50 per 10; $100.00 per 100. 2 yr., 4-5 ft., $1.00 each; $9.00 per 10; $75.00 per 100. 1 yr., from graft, 25c each; $2.00 per 10; $15.00 per 100.

Oregon—Valuable new variety that originated in the State of Oregon. Tree is a rapid grower, very productive, large apples. Attractive fruit, red over yellow, fine flavor. The calyx has the same peculiar shape as the Delicious. Fruit very uniform. Prices; 5-7 ft., $1.00 each; $9.00 per 10. 3½-5 ft., 75c each; $6.00 per 10.

Harmon Sweet—Introduced by us in 1926. Mr. Harmon, the originator, describes the apple as follows: "I consider it a better apple than the Tolman Sweet, richer and more juicy and better keeper. The tree is extremely hardy and vigorous, producing a good crop annually." Prices: 5-7 ft., $1.00 each; $9.00 per 10. 3-5 ft., 75c each; $6.00 per 10.

SUMMER APPLES

Chenango Strawberry, Early Harvest, Early Strawberry, Golden Sweet, Red Astrachan, Sweet Bough, Williams' Early Red, Yellow Transparent.

WINTER APPLES

Baldwin, Ben Davis, Cortland, Delicious, Golden Russet, Grimes' Golden, Hubbardston's Nonesuch, Jonathan, King of Tompkins County, Maiden Blush, Maine Seedling, McIntosh Red, N. W. Greening, Northern Spy, Rhode Island Greening, Rome Beauty, Roxbury Russet, Stayman's Winesap, Smokehouse, Spitzenburgh, Stark, Sutton Beauty, Tolman Sweet, Wagener, Winesap, Winter Banana, Yellow Belleflower, York Imperial.

THE OSWEGO APPLE

AUTUMN APPLES

Alexander, Bailey Sweet, Duchess, Fall Pippin, Fameuse, Gravenstein, Greasy Pippin (Ortley), Grandmother's Pie Apple (Rib. Pippin), Pound Sweet, St. Lawrence, Twenty Ounce, Wealthy.

CRAB APPLE

Hyslop and Transcendent.

APPLE SCIONS FOR GRAFTING

We can supply the scions of the most popular varieties of apples at 40c per 10; $2.50 per 100. Oswego, Oregon, Harmon Sweet, St. Lawrence, McIntosh and Cortland, 50c per 10; $3.00 per 100.

GRAFTING WAX

Made of best materials from recipe furnished by the Department of Horticulture, Syracuse University. Prices: ¼ lb., 30c; ½ lb., 45c; 1 lb., 75c.

FRUITING SIZE COLLECTION

Standard Trees, 6-8 Feet, $1.25 each;

4 for $4.60

1 Northern Spy	1 McIntosh Red
1 Winter Banana	1 Duchess

NOTE: Duchess trees bore last season in the nursery row.

FARMER'S APPLE COLLECTION

5 Standard Trees, 5-7 Feet

1 Oregon	1 Harmon Sweet
1 Baldwin	1 St. Lawrence
	1 Yellow Transparent

Value, $4.25—Special Prices, $3.25

PRICES OF FARMER'S STANDARD APPLE TREES

All Varieties Except Oswego, Oregon and Harmon Sweet.

Size		Each	10	100
Large	5-7 Feet	$0.75	$6.50	$55.00
Medium	3½-5 Feet	.55	4.50	35.00
Small	1-Year Grafts	.25	2.00	15.00

Extra Large, Transplanted Trees, 3 and 4-Yr., $1.00 each; $9.00 per 10.

OREGON APPLE

BURBANK PLUM—A Leading Market Variety

Plum Trees

European Varieties—Bradshaw, Fellenberg (Italian Prune), German Prune, French Prune, Imperial Gage, Lombard, Moore's Arctic, Monarch, Niagara, Reine Claude (Green Gage), Shipper's Pride, Shropshire Damson, Yellow Egg, York State Prune.

Japanese Varieties — Abundance, Burbank, Red June, Satsuma, Wickson.

Prof. Hansen Hybrids—Hanska, Opata, Stella.

Price of Farmer's Plum Trees — Large, 5-7 ft., 85c each; $6.50 per 10; $45.00 per 100.

PLUM TREE COLI

4 Full Size, 2-Year Tre
1 Burbank
1 German Prune
Catalog Price, $3.40—Collec

Pear Tr

Summer Varieties—Bartlett, (Wilder.

Autumn Varieties—Buerre Bo Duchess (Duchess d'Angoulem Garber, Seckel, Sheldon, Wor Beauty.

Winter Varieties—Kieffer, La Price of Farmer's Standard Pea ft., 90c each; $8.00 per 10;

STANDARD PEAR C

4 Full Size, 2-Year Tre
1 Bartlett
1 Clapp's Favorite
Catalog Price, $3.60—Collec

Cherry T

Sour Varieties—Baldwin, Earl Morello, May Duke, Montmoren Price, Sour Cherries—Large, 5-7 per 10; $65.00 p Sweet Varieties—Bing, Black Wood, Lambert, Napoleon, : Windsor.

Price, Sweet Cherries, Large 5-7 per 10.

Peach T

Varieties—Belle of Georgia, Crawford Early, Crawford L Greensboro, J. H. Hale, Niagar ter, Stump the World.

Price of Peach Trees, Large, 4- per 10; $35.00 per 100. 55c each; $4.50 per 10; {

BARGAIN PEACH C

4 Full Size, 4-5 Ft. Tree
1 Greensboro
1 Crawford Early
Catalog Price, $2.60—Colle

BARTLETT PEAR

Dwarf Fruit Trees

oduce Larger Fruit in Smaller Space and in Less Time Than Standard Trees.

DWARF trees are extremely desirable for the home orchard, especially in the city or village garden where space is limit-. The usual planting distance is 8 to 12 et, but both dwarf apple and dwarf pear es may be set 4 to 5 feet apart in hedge ws. Among the other important advan- ges is the early bearing habit. Same var- ies will bear full sized fruits the second ar after planting, and produce more fruit a given space than standard trees. Many owers contend that the fruit is larger and erages better quality than that produced standard trees. The low growing habit ot only makes the dwarf tree convenient to each and care for, but also it is possible to ow small fruits and vegetables in the same rden.

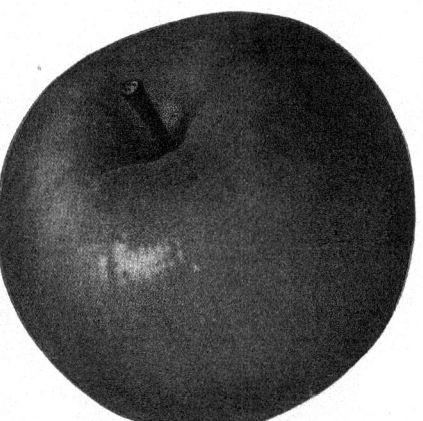

CORTLAND APPLE

Dwarf Cortland Apple

Dwarf Cortland Apple — An improved McIntosh de- veloped by the N. Y. S. Agr. Experiment Station. The color is superior to the McIntosh and the size is about the same. It ripens somewhat later and can be kept longer in the cellar. The flesh is crisp, fine-grained and much like the parent in flavor. The fruit hangs on the tree better than that of the McIntosh. We have a limited number of well rooted, thrifty trees, 3 years old, budded on imported stocks. This is your opportunity to test the Cortland without wait- ing for standard trees to bear. **Price: Dwarf Cortland, 3 yr., 4½-5½ ft., well branched, $1.00 each; $9.00 per 10.**

DWARF APPLES

Autumn Strawberry, Baldwin, Chenango Strawberry, Cort- land, Delicious, Duchess, Early Harvest, Early Strawberry, Fameuse (Snow), Gravenstein, Golden Sweet, Golden Rus- set, Grimes Golden Pippin, King, Lady, Liveland Raspber- ry, Maiden Blush, McIntosh Red, Northern Spy, Red As- trachan, R. I. Greening, Rome Beauty, Stayman's Winesap, Sweet Bough, Wealthy, Yellow Transparent. **Price: Farm- er's Dwarf Apple Trees (Except Cortland), 2 yr., 4-5 ft., well branched, 90c each; $8.50 per 10.**

DWARF PEARS

Bartlett, Bar-Seckel, Buerre de Anjou, Cayuga, Clapp's Favorite, Comice, Dana Hovey, Dr. Reeder, Duchess, Flem- ish Beauty, Kieffer, Idaho, Louise Bonne, Osband, Seckel, Souvenir, Vermont Beauty, Wilder, Worden-Seckel. **Price: Farmer's Dwarf Pear Trees, 2 yr., 4-5 ft., well branched, 80c each; $7.50 per 10.**

OUR CHOICE COLLECTION

Shade and Ornamental Trees

SHADE trees have a very important place in the layout of the home grounds. No landscape planting is complete without trees to frame the view. They add prominence and beauty to the home and provide shade wherever it is needed. "Plant a tree wherever it will serve a desired purpose."

Ash, European Mountain—A very attractive, round-headed tree growing 20-30 feet high, with light green foliage, showy clusters of bright red fruit. 6-8 ft., $2.00 each.

Birch, Cut-Leaf Weeping—A beautiful tree for the lawn, with white bark, drooping branches and finely cut foliage. 6-8 ft., $4.00 each.

Birch, European White—A fine tree with silvery white bark and spray-like branches. Very effective among tall evergreens. 6-8 ft., $2.00 each.

Catalpa Bungei (Umbrella Catalpa)—An excellent tree for small lawns and formal plantings. The round, compact heads remain symmetrical without pruning. The leaves are heart-shaped in a deep, glossy green. 5-6 ft., $2.00; 6-8 ft., $3.00 each.

Crab, Bechtel's Flowering — Bears great quantities of double pink flowers, resembling miniature roses. Fragrant. 3-4 ft., $1.25 each.

Crab, Floribunda—One of the best of the early spring flowering trees. Flowers rose colored and produced in great abundance. 4-5 ft., $1.50 each.

Elm, American—The king of American shade trees. A tall, graceful, wide-spreading tree with outward curving and pendulous branches. A favorite avenue tree. 6-8 ft., $1.00; 8-10 ft., $1.50 each.

JAPANESE FLOWERING CHERRY

Elm, Camperdown (Weeping Elm)—A form of the Scotch Elm, with curving, pendulous branches, the limbs often spreading horizontally. Very ornamental and useful as an arbor on a lawn. 5-7 ft., $4.50 each.

Flowering Cherry, Japanese—Double pink blossoms completely cover the slender branches before the leaves appear. A delightful addition to any planting. 3-4 ft., $3.00 each.

Horse Chestnut—White flowers produced in showy clusters in abundance. 4-5 ft., $1.50 each.

Linden, American — A stately tree with large, smooth leaves and showy yellow flowers. Fragrant. A rapidly growing tree, with round, dense head. 6-8 ft., $2.50 each.

Maple, Norway — We consider this the best all round shade tree. Grows a compact, rounded head with deep green foliage. The tree is clean, perfectly hardy and free from disease. A vigorous grower, reaching a height of 50-60 feet at maturity. Unsurpassed for park, avenue or lawn planting. 6-8 ft., $2.25; 8-10 ft., $3.00 each.

Maple, Silver Leaf — One of the fastest growing trees, valuable where quick shade is desired. Leaves silvery underneath and light green above. 8-10 ft., $1.25 each; $10.00 per 10. 6-8 ft., 85c each; $7.50 per 10.

CUT-LEAF WEEPING BIRCH

20

Shade and Ornamental Trees

Maple, Schwedler's Purple Leaf—A variety of the Norway Maple with reddish-purple foliage turning to bronze in autumn. Very ornamental, especially in contrast with the green foliage of other varieties. 8-10 ft., $3.50 each.

Maple, Wier's Cut-Leaf — A weeping form with deeply cut leaves. A vigorous grower. 6-8 ft., $1.75 each.

Mulberry, Tea's Weeping—One of the very best of small weeping lawn trees. Slender, arching branches droop to the ground. Foliage dense, deep green and attractive. 5-6 ft., $3.50 each.

Mulberry, Russian—A hardy, rapid growing tree. Foliage abundant; fruits attractive to birds. 5-7 ft., $1.00 each.

Oriental Plane—A majestic tree in summer with its large head of bright green, heart-shaped foliage. Attractive also in winter with its smooth creamy-white bark, mottled by dark blotches of older bark which peels off in thin plates. Good for park, avenue or large lawn. Tolerant to smoky conditions, moist soils and seaside planting. 6-8 ft., $1.75 each.

Poplar, Carolina — Very rapid, luxuriant grower, probably the fastest growing shade tree. Useful as windbreak, screen, or for quick shade. Thrives under practically any conditions. 6-8 ft., 60c each; $5.00 per 10. 8-10 ft., 75c each; $6.50 per 10. 10-12 ft., $1.00 each; $9.00 per 10.

Poplar, Lombardy—A very picturesque tree, narrow and pyramidal in growth. Useful as a tall screen, for groups in parks or cemeteries, or for formal effects. 6-8 ft., 75c each; $7.00 per 10. 8-10 ft., $1.25 each; $11.50 per 10. 10-12 ft., $1.75 each; $16.50 per 10.

NORWAY MAPLE

Plum, Double Flowering—A charming little lawn tree growing to about six feet. In the early spring before the leaves appear the branches are covered with a profusion of double rose flowers; individual blossom about one inch across. A cheery spot of color in any landscape. 3-4 ft., $1.25 each.

Plum, Purple Leaved—A striking little tree with dark purple branches. Leaves are glossy crimson when young, changing to dark purple and retain this color until they drop in the fall. Flowers small, white, single, covering the tree in May. 3-4 ft., $1.00; 5-6 ft., $1.50 each.

Thorn, Paul's Double Scarlet—A showy and pretty tree with numerous carmine red flowers. Red fruits very ornamental. Will thrive anywhere. 5-6 ft., $2.25 each.

Strawberry Tree (Euonymous)—A small, upright growing tree with good foliage and scarlet berries in autumn. 4-5 ft., $1.00 each.

Willow, Golden—A very pretty tree with golden-

SPIRAEA VAN HOUTTEI
1½-2 ft., 25c; 2-3 ft., 50c;
3-4 ft., 75c

Japanese Barberry

he Most Beautiful, the Most Satisfactory, the Most Economical Hedge Plant

any Times During the Season We Are Asked, "What Is the Best edge Plant?" . Almost Invariably We Answer, "Japanese Barry," Because—

JAPANESE BARBERRY IS BEAUTIFUL THE YEAR AROUND

In early spring the new leaves are a soft shade of light green; in mmer they turn to a dark glossy green; later, as fall approaches, ey assume striking copper, gold and bronze-red hues. Still more lor is added by the brilliant scarlet berries, which stand out in arp contrast against the dull gray branches and the winter snow.

THE MOST SATISFACTORY HEDGE UNDER AVERAGE CONDITIONS

Japanese Barberry is perfectly hardy; in fact, we have never en any indication of winter injury even to the very tips of the oung branchlets. It will stand pruning at any time of the season, nd may be maintained in any form, either as a clipped hedge or a specimen plant. Because it forms a compact hedge anywhere —in the sun or shade, rich or poor soil, hot or cold climate, we ll Japanese Barberry the World's Most Practical Hedge.

THE MOST ECONOMICAL HEDGE FOR ALL PURPOSES

The first cost is not prohibitive, and once planted a Barberry edge will last forever, if properly maintained. It will provide a ving fence for parks, golf links, cemeteries, and around public r private properties. It fulfills all of the requirements of a board r iron fence, and presents a much more pleasing appearance. The tiff spines on the branches provide a barrier that will turn away he most aggressive trespassers. Japanese Barberry may be used n the foundation planting in front of taller shrubs, along the order planting, on terraces or slopes, in masses at corners, or as a edge along the sidewalk, driveway or property line.

PRICED LOW FOR FIRST QUALITY STOCK

The plants are priced on a basis of quality, age and size. Our tock is healthy, exceptionally heavy rooted and carefully graded. We guarantee our grades to be as specified, and if in any instance he customer is not satisfied we will return the full purchase price. Barberry plants should be set 9-18 inches apart, depending upon he size that you purchase.

JAPAN BARBERRY HEDGE
(See Prices Opposite)

	Each	10	100
Five-year specimens, 3-4 ft.	$0.60	$5.00	
Four-year specimens, 3-3½ ft.	.50	4.00	$30.00
Three-year specimens, 2½-3 ft.	.40	3.00	22.00
Three-year specimens, 1½-2 ft.	.30	2.50	17.50
Two-year specimens, 9-18 in.	.20	1.50	10.00

New Red Leaved Japanese Barberry—A recent and valuable introduction in the shrub line. It not only has all the qualities of the Japanese Barberry, but the outstanding characteristic of this new variety is the glossy, bronze-red foliage. The leaves do not lose their color, but become more brilliant as the season advances. Should be set in full sunlight. Prices: 1-year, 75c each; $6.00 per 10. 2-year, $1.00 each; $8.00 per 10.

OTHER HEDGES

Lodense Privet—A comparatively recent introduction. Forms a low, compact, hedge or border. Foliage dark, glossy green. Stands shearing well, hardy. 15-18 in., 3 yrs., 40c each; $3.50 per 10; $28.00 per 100. 12-15 in., 2 yrs., 30c each; $2.50 per 10; $18.00 per 100. 16-18 in., 2 yrs., 20c each; $1.50 per 10; $12.00 per 100.

Amoor River Privet—Extremely hardy northern variety similar in habits to California Privet. 3-4 ft., 25c each; $2.00 per 10; $15.00 per 100. 2-3 ft., 20c each; $1.50 per 10; $12.00 per 100. 18-24 in., 15c each; $1.20 per 10; $9.00 per 100.

Ibota Privet—Large white flowers; very fragrant. 3-4 ft., 40c each; $3.00 per 10; $24.00 per 100. 2-3 ft., 30c each; $2.00 per 10; $16.00 per 100. 18-24 in., 20c each; $1.50 per 10; $12.00 per 100.

California Privet—3-4 ft., 20c each; $1.50 per 10; $10.00 per 100. 2-3 ft., 15c each; $1.20 per 10; $8.00 per 100. 18-24 in., 10c each; 80c per 10; $6.00 per 100.

Buckthorn—A good plant for tall hedges or windbreaks. Thrives under adverse conditions. Prices: large plants, 3-4 ft., 50c each; $4.00 per 10.

NEW RED-LEAVED JAPANESE DWARF BARBERRY
(See Prices Opposite)

23

Flowering Shrubs

NEW VIRGINALIS
Mock Orange

HOME is more than four square walls; even the most costly mansion standing on a barren lot is cold and uninviting. The modest cottage sheltered by shade trees, surrounded by a green lawn, softened by shrub masses and clinging vines, invites us within. Surely, "It's not a home until it's planted."

In arranging a planting, always maintain an open lawn, keeping the plants near the border of the lot and against the foundation of the buildings. The border planting may be arranged in rather heavy masses, thereby attaining somewhat of a privacy on your grounds, but defining the limits of the property. Use a variety of kinds, but enough of one type in a place to produce a definite effect of light, shade, color, flower or fruit.

Shrubs Tolerant to Shade — Japanese Barberry, Dogwoods, Honeysuckle, Mock Orange, Common Snowball, Coralberry, Snowberry, Hydrangea arborescens, Shadbush, High Bush Cranberry, Deutzia, Privet.

Low Growing Shrubs—Japanese Barberry, Red-leaved Japanese Barberry, Dwarf Deutzia, Lemoine's Deutzia, Spirea Thunbergi, Spirea Anthony Waterer, Hydrangea Hills of Snow.

Medium Growing Shrubs — Deutzia Pride of Rochester, Hydrangea P. G., Spirea Van Houttei, Coralberry, Snowberry, Weigela, Japan Snowball, Golden Bell, White Kerria.

Tall Growing Shrubs for Corners and Screen Planting—Althea, Bush Honeysuckles, Mock Orange, Common Snowball, Dogwoods, Common Lilac, High Bush Cranberry.

HONEYSUCKLE BUSH

Chrysantha—Yellow flowers, red fruit. 2-3 ft., 50c; 3-4 ft., 75c each.

Morrow's—Upright and dense in growth. Numerous white flowers in May and June, followed by bright red fruit from August until winter. 2-3 ft., 50c; 3-4 ft., 75c each.

Tartarian—A very useful and attractive shrub with an abundance of fragrant flowers in spring, followed by red berries in autumn. Colors, pink or white. 2-3 ft., 50c; 3-4 ft., 75c each.

HYDRANGEA

Arborescens Sterilis (Hills of Snow or Snowball Hydrangea) —White flowers borne in great masses, practically covering the shrub. June and July. 1½-2 ft., 50c; 2-3 ft., 75c each.

Paniculata Grandiflora (Large Flowered Hydrangea)—The popular variety which produces immense cone-shaped heads of white flowers, changing to bronze and lasting the balance of the season. Bush form, 1½-2 ft., 40c; 2-3 ft., 60c; 3-4 ft., 80c each. Extra select plants, $1.00 each.

Tree Hydrangea—2-3 ft., $1.00; 3-4 ft., $1.50; 4-5 ft., $2.00; 5-6 ft., $2.50 each. All exceptionally heavy rooted and well branched.

Japan Quince (Cydonia)—Large scarlet flowers produced in masses. Foliage deep and glossy green. Good in hedges or for massing in the shrubbery border. 1½-2 ft., 50c each; $4.00 per 10. 2-3 ft., 75c each; $6.00 per 10.

LILAC

Purple Lilac—The familiar, old-fashioned European lilac with deep purple flowers. Useful in tall hedges or screens. 2-3 ft., 50c each; $4.50 per 10. 3-4 ft., 75c each; $6.50 per 10.

White Lilac—A white form of the preceding. Same price.

Almond, Flowering—Double blossoms like small roses completely cover the shrub in May. White or pink. 2-3 ft., 75c; 3-4 ft., $1.00 each.

Althea or Rose of Sharon—Double flowers in colors, pink, purple, red or white. One of the few hardy shrubs to bloom in August and September. 2-3 ft., 50c; 3-4 ft., 75c each.

Barberry—See hedge plants, page 23.

Buckthorn—See hedge plants, page 23.

Butterfly Bush, Everblooming Summer Lilac—A rapid grower that produces an abundance of blooms the first season. Panicles of beautiful lilac-colored flowers attract the butterflies in great numbers. Medium size, 50c; selected heavy root plants, 75c each.

Calycanthus, Carolina Allspice — Chocolate-brown flowers about 3 inches across and shaped like pineapples. Flowers and bark sweet-scented; foliage deep, glossy green. 2-3 ft., 75c each.

Coralberry, or Indian Currant—Small pink flowers in July. Spreading in habit; long, slender branches bending gracefully toward the ground, covered in autumn and winter with racemes of currant-like fruit. Useful for banks and dry spots. 2-3 ft., 50c; 3-4 ft., 75c each.

DEUTZIA

Gracilis, Dwarf Deutzia—A very useful low-growing shrub; uniform and dense in growth. Numerous flowers, fragrant, produced in May and June on slender, arching branches. Colors, pink or white. Medium size, 50c; large, 75c each.

Lemoine's Deutzia — Extra large white flowers, in great panicles. Blooms in June. 1½-2 ft., 50c each.

DOGWOOD

Elegantissima, Variegated Dogwood—A pretty dwarf shrub with blood-red bark and white and green foliage. White blossoms in June. 1½-2 ft., 50c; 2-3 ft., 75c each.

Siberica—Cream-colored flowers in June, light blue fruits. Bark bright red in winter. 2-3 ft., 50c; 3-4 ft., 75c each.

Sanguinea, Red Osier—White flowers in June followed by black fruits. Branches upright and spreading; bark red. Good for wet places. 2-3 ft., 50c; 3-4 ft., 75c each.

Elderberry, Adam's Improved—See page 40.

Golden Leaved Elder—Foliage bright yellow; white flowers in large, flat, showy clusters produced in July. Medium plants, 50c; extra large, 75c each.

False Indigo (Amorpha)—Very ornamental. Large spikes of violet-purple flowers, pea-shaped, in narrow, drooping clusters. 3-4 ft., 75c each.

Golden Bell (Forsythia)—Bright yellow, bell-shaped flowers in April before the leaves appear. 3-4 ft., 60c each.

SPECIAL OFFER
You May Select From This Catalog
ANY TEN 50c SHRUBS FOR $4.50
ANY TEN 75c SHRUBS FOR $6.50

HYBRID LILACS

The French Budded Lilacs are fast taking the place of the common lilac as the people are beginning to know them. This is because of the size and greater range of color and season of bloom. The French Hybrids often blossom the same year they are set, while the common lilac may not bloom for several years.

Charles X—Extra large flower panicles, deep red in color. A rapid grower.

Marie Legraye—Large trusses of white flowers. One of the very finest.

President Grevy—Very large, double, rose-lilac flowers. A favorite.

24

Flowering Shrubs

HYDRANGEA ARBORESCENS—Hills of Snow

HYBRID LILACS

Alphonse Lavalle—Double. Blue shading to violet in extra large panicles.

Chas. Joly—Dark reddish-purple. Large, double flowers.

Mad. Lemoine—Double, pure white. A superb variety.

Michael Buchner—A dwarf variety. Pale lilac flowers, very double.

Souv. d' Ludwig Spaeth—Very large, single, dark purple flowers. The finest variety on our grounds. Price, all varieties, 2-3 ft., $1.00 per tree.

MOCK ORANGE (Syringa)

Virginalis, The New Mock Orange—A choice, new variety producing large, creamy-white flowers, double and delightfully fragrant. Flowers in May and June and intermittently until fall. 3-4 ft., $1.00 each.

Golden Syringa—A compact shrub with brilliant yellow foliage which lasts throughout the summer. White flowers in June. Good for contrast against other shrubs. Medium, 60c; large, 75c each.

Coronarius (Garland Syringa)—The well known Syringa with pure white and highly scented flowers. An excellent shrub for the border. 2-3 ft., 50c; 3-4 ft., 75c each.

Grandiflorus (Large Flowered Mock Orange)—Very showy white flowers. Grows 10-15 feet. Very good for tall hedge or screens. 2-3 ft., 50c; 3-4 ft., 75c each.

SPIREA

Van Houtte (Bridal Wreath)—One of the most handsome and useful of the hardy shrubs, and the best of the spireas. Large clusters of white flowers completely cover the arching branches. Foliage dense, deep green. 1½-2 ft., 25c each; $2.00 per 10. 2-3 ft., 50c each; $4.00 per 10. 3-4 ft., 75c each, $6.00 per 10.

Prunifolia, True Bridal Wreath—Flowers about ¼-inch across in dense racemes along the upright branches. A pretty shrub with dark green, shining foliage. Requires partial protection until established. 2-3 ft., 75c each; $6.00 per 10.

Anthony Waterer — One of the most useful low growing shrubs. Produces an abundance of bright crimson flowers in flat clusters. If the flowers are cut when they fade, the shrub will continue to bloom until frost. 15-18 in., 50c each; $4.00 per 10. 2 ft., 75c each; $6.00 per 10.

Thunbergi—Very early shrub to flower. Foliage fine, delicate, light green in color. White flowers in long, close racemes in April and May. 2-3 ft., 60c each; 3-4 ft., 75c each.

Golden-leaved Spirea—A strong growing shrub with bright yellow foliage and showy clusters of flowers about 3 inches across. Large plants, 4 ft., 50c each; $4.00 per 10.

Froebeli—Bright crimson flowers resembling Anthony Waterer. 2-3 ft., 50c each.

Billardi—Dense spikes of bright pink flowers about 6 inches long in July and August. 3 ft., 50c each.

Sorbifolia — Leaves like Mountain Ash. Large spikes of white flowers in July and August. 4 ft., 60c each.

Callosa Rosea—Similar to Anthony Waterer, but taller in growth. 2-3 ft., 50c each.

Pearl Bush (Exochorda)—A splendid shrub producing pearl-like buds which open in pure white flowers. 1½ inches across in racemes of 4 and 5. Price: 3 ft., 75c each.

Snowberry—An upright shrub, valued for its waxy, showy berries in autumn. Small pink flowers in July. 2-3 ft., 50c; 3-4 ft., 75c each.

Sumach, Cutleaf—Pretty shrub, leaflets deeply cut, fern-like. Turns a beautiful crimson in autumn. 3-4 ft., 75c each.

Shadbush or Juneberry (Amelanchier)—White flowers in May. Fruits purplish, ornamental and edible. 2-3 ft., 75c each.

VIBURNUM

Plicatum, Japan Snowball—A strong growing shrub with large, dark green leaves. Flowers in round heads of pure white in June. Most satisfactory of snowballs because of its freedom from the attacks of plant lice. Medium size, 75c each; large, $1.00 each.

Opulus, High Bush Cranberry—Clusters of red fruit, resembling cranberries, hang on the bush from August well into the winter. 2-3 ft., 75c each.

Opulus Sterilis, Common Snowball—The old-fashioned snowball, producing immense heads of snowy-white flowers in June. 3 ft., 75c each.

Tamarix, African Tamarisk—Feathery light green foliage and spreading branches gives oriental effect. Pink flowers along the branches before the leaves appear. 3 ft., 60c each.

WEIGELA

Rosea—One of the finest shrubs in cultivation. Pink flowers in abundance. 2-3 ft., 50c each; $4.00 per 10. 3-4 ft., 75c each; $6.00 per 10.

Rosea Purpureis—Light pink flowers. Rich bronzy-purple foliage. 2-3 ft., 75c each.

Eva Rathke—Crimson flowers, very handsome and fragrant; free flowering and almost everblooming. 1½-2 ft., 50c each; $4.00 per 10. 2-3 ft., 75c each; $6.00 per 10.

Nana Variegata—Dense and dwarf in habit: leaves distinctly margined orange-yellow. Rose-colored flowers in June. 2-3 ft., 75c; 3-4 ft., $1.00 each.

Candida, White Weigela—Flowers extra large and showy. Requires partial protection until well established. 2-3 ft., 75c; 3-4 ft., $1.00 each.

Lilac Weigela—3 ft., 60c each.

White Kerria (Rhodotypos)—Very ornamental. Single white flowers, 1½ inches across, in May and June, followed by conspicuous, shiny black fruits in autumn and winter. 2-3 ft., 75c; 3-4 ft., $1.00 each.

If you are planning to do any extensive planting around your home, send us your list of plants, and we will be pleased to quote special quantity prices.

culture produces hardy, vigorous plants
ll developed root systems. Taken from
d after the wood and bark have ripened
hey have stored-up energy, ready to pro-
lth of blossoms within a few weeks.
isfactory method of winter protection
mounding earth around each plant to a
3-12 inches. Then the surface should be
ith 6 inches of coarse litter or straw.

v and Rare Roses

ith Helen—The most striking pink rose of re-
Enormous, very double, pure pink blooms, con-
luced. Strong growth. $1.50 each.

Feu—Long pointed buds, full double, gorgeous
flowers, changing to coral pink. $1.00 each.

Hollande—Flowers brilliant dark red, delicious-
l. Growth vigorous, upright. A rose with a
. $2.00 each.

oymans — Large, deep orange-yellow flowers,
tinged apricot. $2.00 each.

der—Very large blooms of cream-yellow, show-
of rich apricot when fully open. Sweetly scent-
ie on excellent stems. $1.50 each.

rlemont—Splendid pointed buds and pointed
vivid scarlet-rose which does not fade as many
ne of the outstanding new roses. $1.50 each.

Page Roberts—A gorgeous rose, developing to
magnificence in size, color and fragrance. Gold-
ind cream in the inside of the flower, stained
dull red on the outside. $2.00 each.

Los Angeles—Luminous flame-pink like the
Pointed form, with good substance and delicious
More vigorous than the bush form. $1.00 each.

otendorst—A pink sport of the F. J. Grooten-
larger flowers of a beautiful shell-pink. A vig-
gy shrub, absolutely hardy, and in flower all
$1.25 each.

NEW PINK GROOTENI

PAUL'S SCARLET
Most Popular Climbing Rose

Climbing

Price, All Varieties, Unless Oth
1, 60c each; 3-Yea

American Pillar—Single rosy-pink
Aviateur Bleriot—One of the yel
yellow.

Bess Lovett—One of the very best
ers of Hybrid Tea size. Plant st
disease.

Blue Rambler—Magenta-blue in c
Climbing American Beauty—Rose
Crimson Rambler—Deep crimson.
Dorothy Perkins—Shell-pink.
Dr. Van Fleet—Rich shell-pink.
Emily Gray—Most dependable y
year, 75c; 3-year, $1.00 each.
Excelsa (Red Dorothy Perkins)—An
edges of the petals a little lighter, produ
Gardenia—Buds bright yellow, flowe:
Hiawatha—Crimson, with white eye.
Mary Lovett—Large, handsome flo
sweet scented. Resembles Dr. Van Flee
Mary Wallace—Semi-double, rose-pink
New.
Paul's Scarlet Climber—Vivid scarlet,
Silver Moon—Silvery-white with yello
Tausendschon (Thousand Beauties)—
white to deep pink.
White Dorothy Perkins—Pure white.

F. J. GROOTENDORST—TF
Bright crimson flowers in clusters,
fully fringed, resembling carnations.
ously from early spring to frost. Fc
disease. An extremely hardy plant, val
and particularly adapted for hedges a
strong 2-year plants, 75c each; $7.00 p

26

machinery or concocted by mixing up a batch of chemicals.

RICA'S FAVORITE COLLECTION
OST POPULAR DOZEN BY VOTE OF THE AMERICAN ROSE SOCIETY

OIUS PERNET   RED RADIANCE   LOS ANGELES

O HERRIOT   OPHELIA   DUCHESS OF WELLINGTON

Farmer's Select Roses

HYBRID TEAS BLOOM FROM JUNE TO FROST

Price, All Hybrid Teas, Unless Otherwise Noted, 2-Year No. 1, 80c each; 3-Year, $1.00 each.

Alexander Hill Gray—Pale lemon-yellow. Deeper in center.

Betty Uprichard—Copper-red buds, semi-double; orange-carmine on outside of petals, showing light salmon reflexes.

Edel—Large; pure ivory-white; lovely globular form. A superb sort which should be in all collections of white roses.

Independence Day—Flaming yellow buds, shaded copper and brown, opening to light orange-pink.

Killarney Queen—Cerise-pink; double and more distinct than either Killarney or Killarney Brilliant.

Lady Alice Stanley—Outside of petals coral-pink, inside pale flesh-pink. One of the best dependable roses for cutting.

Lady Ursula—Light pink merging to yellow base. Tremendous growth, and very free flowering.

Mme. Jules Bouche—Superb white flowers, shaded blush at center. Probably the best white bedding rose in the Hybrid Teas. Price, $1.00 each.

Mme. Leon Pain—Silvery flesh-pink, center yellowish orange. Exceeded in blooming by no rose equal to it in beauty.

Mrs. H. Prentiss Nichols—Massive dark pink blooms. One of the best new American roses.

William R. Smith—Creamy white, suffused with bright rose-pink. One of the hardiest Tea Roses for the North.

Betty—Coppery-rose, overspread with golden yellow.

Cheerful—Bright pink with sunny glow.

Columbia—Lively pink, shading darker at maturity.

Duchess of Wellington—Intense saffron-yellow, stained rich crimson, changing to deep coppery-yellow.

Etoile de France—Velvety crimson, with cerise center.

General McArthur—Brilliant crimson-scarlet.

Golden Emblem—Rich deep golden-yellow.

Gruss an Teplitz—Scarlet, constantly in bloom.

Hadley—Velvety crimson.

H. V. Machin—Black-grained scarlet-crimson.

J. L. Mock—Outside of petals deep pink, inside silvery-rose.

Kaiserin Augusta Victoria—White; fine form.

Lady Ashtown—Shining pink shading to yellow.

Lady Hillingdon—Deep apricot-yellow.

Lieutenant Chaure—Velvety red, shaded garnet.

Los Angeles — Luminous flame pink, toned coral, shaded translucent gold at base of petals.

Mme. Butterfly—Bright pink, apricot and gold.

Mme. Caroline Testout—Rich pink.

Mme. Edouard Herriot—Coral-red, shaded yellow and scarlet.

Miss Lolita Armour—Coral, golden and coppery-yellow.

Mrs. Aaron Ward—Yellow, sometimes shaded salmon and rose.

Ophelia—Salmon-flesh, shaded rose.

Radiance—Carmine-pink, yellow at base of petals.

Red Radiance—Dazzling crimson-scarlet.

Souvenir de Claudius Pernet—New, sunflower-yellow. Price, 2-year, 90c; 3-year, $1.10 each.

Souvenir de Georges Pernet—Brick-red buds opening terra-cotta pink.

Sunburst—Rich yellow, shaded coppery-orange.

White Killarney—Waxy-white.

William F. Dreer—Shell-pink, yellow at base.

Willowmere—Shrimp-pink, shaded yellow at center.

HYBRID PERPETUAL OR JUNE ROSES

Price, All Varieties, 2-Year, 75c; 3-Year, 95c each.

Alfred Colomb—Crimson. Full, finely shaped flowers.

Anne de Diesbach—Pink, long pointed buds.

Captain Hayward—Bright scarlet, large flowers.

Fisher Holmes—Magnificent reddish scarlet beneath a black, velvety sheen.

Frau Karl Druschki—The best white rose of any class. Almost a constant bloomer.

General Jacqueminot—Bright crimson. Very free blooming.

George Arends (Pink Frau Karl Druschki)—The best clear pink rose.

Harrison's Yellow—Deep golden-yellow.

Hugh Dickson—Large, brilliant scarlet blooms, full and fragrant. Established plants almost everblooming.

FRAU KARL DRUSCHKI

Magna Charta—Rosy-pink, tinted carmine.

Margaret Dickson—White with flesh center.

Marshall P. Wilder—Crimson, full; extra large.

Mrs. John Laing—Soft pink, very fragrant. Blooms throughout season.

Paul Neyron—Pink, shading to rose.

Prince Camille de Rohan—Deep maroon of velvety texture.

Soliel d'Or—Reddish-gold, shaded with orange.

Ulrich Brunner—Bright carmine-red, cup-shaped flowers. An old favorite.

MOSS ROSES

Prices: 3-year, $1.00; 2-year, 75c

Blanche Moreau—Large, pure white, very fragrant.

Princess Adelaide—Very large, bright rosy-pink, moderately fragrant.

DWARF POLYANTHA OR "BABY RAMBLERS"

The Polyanthas are a distinct and charming class of roses. All summer they produce an abundance of clusters of small, perfectly formed flowers. The buds and flowers make ideal boutonnieres.

Varieties: Echo — pink; Katherina Zeimet — white; Erna Teschendorff—carmine-red. 2-year, 75c each; $6.00 per 10.

RUGOSA AND HYBRID RUGOSA ROSES

Conrad F. Meyer—Large, double, clear silvery-rose flowers. Strong fragrance. 3-year, $1.00; 2-year, 75c; 1-year, 25c each.

F. J. Grootendorst—Described on page 26.

New Pink Grootendorst—Described on page 26.

Red Japanese Rose (Rugosa Rubra) — 2-year, 75c; 3-year, $1.00 each.

White Japanese Rose (Rugosa Alba)—Same price as above.

HUGONIS
"The Golden Rose of China"

Blooms Early in May, Three Weeks Before Other Roses

This native of China takes first place among the single flowered roses. Clear yellow, delicately fragrant flowers, 2½ inches across, borne so abundantly on gracefully arching branches as to form a continuous band of color. Foliage fine, pale green and distinct, on curious red-tipped twigs. Makes a symmetrical shrub about 6 feet wide and as high when matured. Hardy anywhere in America. Prices: 2-year, $1.00 each; $8.00 per 10. 3-year, $1.25 each; $10.00 per 10.

LUCIDA
"The Shrub Rose"

An extremely hardy rose with large, bright pink flowers. Particularly desirable as a shrub, as the foliage is attractive throughout the season. Prices: 3-year plants, $1.00 each; 2-year plants, 75c each.

28

nental Vines

illy arranged, give the
ome planting. They are
and fragrance of their
d stone walls, porches,
ng near the foundation,
i rich garden soil to a

idbine)—Leaves deep green
n. Good for covering walls,
.-yr. vines, 30c each; $2.50

hi)—Leaves three-lobed and
low in the fall. Vine grows
ices evenly with overlapping
or stone surfaces. Requires
yr. strong roots, 75c each;

of American Ivy. Clings to
ies, 50c each; $4.50 per 10.
s .vine, pure white flowers,
ain on the vine from July to
each; $4.50 per 10.
ll-known, useful vine, with
y free flowering and showy.
ower. 2-yr. vines, 50c each;

r, glossy, dark green leaves,
ed in profusion. Good for
50c each; $4.50 per 10.
'ree bloomer. Very large,
yr. vines, 75c each.

CLEMATIS PANICULATA

Clematis Mad. Edw. Andre — Large flowers a vivid
crimson; borne as freely as Jackmani. 2-yr. vines, 95c
each.
Clematis Duch. of Edinburgh — Large, double, pure
white flowers. June to October. 2-yr. vines, 95c each.
Clematis Ramona—Numerous sky-blue flowers, often
six inches across. June to October. 2-yr. vines, 95c each.
Clematis Henryi—Large, creamy-white flowers, six to
eight petals. July to October. 2-yr. vines, 95c each.
Clematis Coccinea — A bright, scarlet color, heavy
petaled flower; bell-shaped. Long season of bloom. 2-
yr. vines, 75c each.
Clematis Crispi—Deep blue, bell-shaped flowers from
June to October. 2-yr. vines, 75c each.
Bittersweet Vine—A native vine popular for its orange-
yellow, capsuled fruits in autumn. Showy crimson flowers
in racemes. A vigorous grower, with dense, glossy foliage. Strong, 3-yr. vines, 50c each; $4.50 per 10.
Evergreen Bittersweet (Euonymus radicans vegetus)—
A trailing vine with dark, glossy-green leaves. Valuable
as a ground cover under Rhododendrons or other shrubs.
Evergreen. 2-yr. No. 1, 75c each; $6.00 per 10.
Matrimony Vine—Regarded as a climber, but also good
for trellises and to cover stumps or banks. Bears quantities of brilliant crimson berries along gracefully curving
branches. Strong, 2-yr. vines, 60c each; $5.00 per 10.
English Ivy (Hedera Helix)—A good small-leaved ev-

EVERGREENS

EVERGREENS give a feeling of richness to the landscape planting that cannot be produced without them. They are now considered to be the most beautiful and choice of all foliage plants. Evergreens are beautiful throughout the year, and especially in winter when partially covered with snow, and in the spring when the new growth comes out in contrast to the old.

All our evergreens are shipped with a ball of earth and burlapped. Before planting soak the ball in a tub of water, but do not remove the burlap. Soak the ground once a week during the first summer.

Arborvitae, American — The common arborvitae, used extensively in making dense screens and hedges. Foliage bright green above and yellowish underneath. Branches short and horizontal, forming a pyramidal tree. Specimens, 4½-5 ft., $6.50 each. Note: Write for special quantity prices on smaller grades for evergreen hedges.

Arborvitae, Globe—A dwarf-growing type, forming a compact round ball rarely over 2 or 3 feet in diameter. Dense bright green foliage. Recommended for use in front of taller evergreens or for tub planting. Specimens, 15-18 in., $2.50 each; 18-24 in., $3.50 each.

Arborvitae, Golden—Foliage bright yellowish green all through the winter, changing to golden yellow in the spring. Forms a compact, broad pyramid. We have the finest strain of the Golden Arborvitae. Specimens, 2½-3 ft., $4.50 each.

Arborvitae Pyramidal—A most valuable upright evergreen, of dense, compact habit. Foliage light green. Narrow columnar growth. Unsurpassed for formal plantings or for foundation plantings at entrances and corners. Specimens, 12-18 in., $2.50 each; 2½-3 ft., $4.50 each; 3½-4 ft., $6.50 each.

Arborvitae, Siberian — Broadly pyramidal, dense type, with glaucous green foliage. Used in foundation plantings. Specimens, 1½-2 ft., $3.00 each.

Arborvitae, Siberian Globe — A globose form of the preceding. Very desirable. Specimens, 1½-2 ft., $3.50 each.

Juniper, Savin's—An attractive low evergreen, usually not over 3-4 feet in height. Numerous semi-erect branches well clothed with deep green foliage. An excellent tree for rock work or dwarf plantings. Specimens, 1½-2 ft., $3.50 each.

Juniper, Pfitzer's—A very hardy, valuable, spreading variety with beautiful lacy foliage, silvery green in color. Branches spread horizontally, giving a light feathery appearance. Should be included in every foundation planting. Spreads about 3 feet. Specimens, 2-2½ ft., spread, $5.50 each.

Juniper, Tamarix-Leaved—A distinct trailing variety of Savin's. Forms a compact mat about one foot in height and will spread several feet. Fine for massing on slopes. Specimens, 2-2½ ft., $4.00 each.

Juniper, Chinese—One of the finest and hardiest of evergreens. Pyramidal in outline, with silvery-green, scale-like foliage. It retains its dense habit. Specimens, 3-3½ ft., $6.00 each

Juniper, Swedish — A bushy type, columnar in growth. A very handsome small tree. Specimens, 4-5 ft., $6.50 each.

Silver Red Cedar (J. V. glauca)—A vigorous growing form of the Red Cedar, more conspicuous with its silvery-gray foliage. Cone-shaped. A favorite for specimen work. Specimens, 3-3½ ft., $7.00 each.

Cannart Red Cedar — A fine, pyramidal, compact grower of dark green appearance; some of the branches lengthen out and droop, presenting a pretty picture. Specimens, 3-3½ ft., $6.50 each.

Spiny Green Juniper (J. excelsa stricta) — This beautiful variety forms a dense, narrow conical head, and is of a fine glaucous color. Well adapted for foundation plantings or other places where small trees are required. Specimens, 15-18 in., $3.00 each.

Koster's Blue Spruce—The most striking and beautiful of all evergreens. The silvery-blue lustre, perfection in form and symmetry, make this tree extremely popular. All trees grafted and very scarce. Entirely hardy. Specimens, 1½-2 ft., $12.00 each.

30

MIDAL ARBOR VITAE
occidentalis pyramidalis

NORWAY SPRUCE

A graceful evergreen that will grow anywhere. The best variety for the "Living Christmas Tree." Long used for tall screens, windbreaks and trimmed hedges. Admirably adapted for use in window boxes or tubs.

3-4 ft., each, $3.00.

2-3 ft., each, $1.75; 10, $15.00.

1½-2 ft., each, $1.25; 10, $10.00.

1-1½ ft., each, 75c; 10, $6.00.

Special prices on larger quantities by request.

EVERGREENS

Blue Spruce — A wonderful ornamental foliage. Very effective as a lawn specimen. $6.00 each.

Spruce—A handsome tree of symmetrical light green foliage. Very popular as a Specimens, 1½-2 ft., $4.00 each.

Fir — Attains a height of 50-75 feet in Forms a pyramidal tree of dense and habit. Very hardy and one of the best conifers. Price, 3-4 ft., $3.50 each.

r—Bluish-green leaves and handsome coni-. One of the most successful of American

Mugho Pine—The mo for foundation planting. Perfectly hardy. Specim

Scotch Pine—Tree 40 spreading branches, bec and picturesque. Bark 3 ft., $2.50 each.

Carolina Hemlock—R vation. Unique in hab foliage on sweeping pe and better adapted to tr Hemlock. Price, 2-2½

Plume Cypress (Ret.

Lawn Grass Seed

To Produce a Fine Lawn, You Must First Consider the Seed and Buy the Very Best. Start Right by Using These Famous Lawn Grass Mixtures.

Central Park Mixture—Contains several kinds of grasses in correct proportions, which insures good results under the varying conditions during the spring, summer and the fall. The Central Park Mixture contains only the choicest of recleaned seeds, and will produce a thick, velvety turf which remains green through the entire growing season. We have produced beautiful lawns in a single season with Central Park Mixture. One pound will sow 200-250 square feet. Price, 50c per lb., 5 lbs., $2.25; 10 lbs., $4.00.

GERMAN BENTGRASS MIXTURE

For the most fastidious lawn maker, we recommend Creeping Bentgrass as one of the very finest northern grasses. If used without mixing with other grasses it will produce a thick turf of beautiful emerald-green, absolutely uniform in color and texture. Creeping Bentgrass is particularly adapted for the average lawns in New York State, as it thrives in an acid soil. No lime is needed. Not recommended for light, sandy soils. Sow at the rate of one pound to 300-350 square feet. Price: ½ lb., 65c; 1 lb., $1.10; 5 lbs., $5.00; 10 lbs., $9.00.

SHADY NOOK MIXTURE

A combination of varieties tolerant to shade for use under trees or other shady places where other grasses will not grow. Price: 65c per lb.; 5 lbs., $2.75; 10 lbs., $5.00.

20 HARDY FERNS FOR ONLY $4.00

We offer these 20 choice ferns for only $4.00: 8 Ostrich Plume Ferns, 8 Lady Ferns, 4 Marsh Shield Ferns. One-half the collection for $2.50. Any one fern for 50c.

Hardy out-of-door ferns grow best in the shade or half shade and will do well in the border. They are just the thing for the shady place around your house where most flowers will not do so well.

Of all the hardy ferns, the **Ostrich Plume** is perhaps the best as it grows the tallest and fastest of any fern. It often has as many as 15 fronds gracefully arranged, presenting an object more beautiful than many varieties of palms. Under favorable conditions, the fronds grow 4 feet tall.

Lady Fern—Is a distinct, different type from the Ostrich Plume and the Marsh Shield. It is extremely variable, growing in all situations from low, moist woodlands and shaded stream banks to dry woods and bushy clearings, but to develop its best forms, it wants partial shade and a reasonable amount of moisture in the spring.

The **Marsh Shield Fern** (Aspidium Thelypteris) or evergreen wood fern, is especially at home in shade or half shady places. This fern is used quite extensively for forming ground covers under shrubbery and tall trees, also on rocky hillsides in groups. The leathery fronds, 2 to 3 feet, produced early in the spring, are a dark green color with lanceolate twice pinnate blades. In planting ferns set the top of the crown level with or 1 to 2 inches above the ground.

VIRGINIA
Loudon County
March, 15, 1928
I like to get things from you because they are as represented and with proper care, sure to live. I thank you for the good service always given in the last 6 to 8 years I have been dealing with you.
MRS. K. A. KROMER.

FOUNDATION PLANTING OF HARDY FERNS

Garden Roots and Vegetable Plants

ASPARAGUS

Grow it in your own garden and be sure it's fresh. The sparagus grown in the home patch has the real quality, nd anyone who has not tasted it cannot fully appreciate his vegetable. Asparagus may look fine on the market ench. The chances are it has traveled hundreds or thouands of miles to market and the quality is not there.

Culture. Asparagus does well on most any type of soil hat is somewhat elevated so that the water can run off eadily and the frosts will not kill it in early spring. In he small garden, the roots should be set 1 foot apart in ows 3 feet apart. They should be placed in furrows bout 8 to 10 inches deep, but covered at first with only 3 nches of soil above the crown. The remainder of the ɔil may be filled in the trench at intervals as the plants row. Plenty of manure and thorough cultivation are ssential. We advise mulching with coarse manure after the ɔps are cut off in the fall. This may be worked in around he plants in the spring. One of the secrets of keeping bed fruitful over a period of years is to give the plants chance to get a good start before cutting the shoots. We dvise letting the plants grow two years before cutting. here seems to be a difference of opinion in regard to he best age plants to set. Some of the best authorities ecommend 1-year roots; we have the best success with 2 nd 3 and 4-year roots.

MARTHA WASHINGTON ASPARAGUS

The Rust-Resisting Martha Washington—This new variety introduced by the U. S. Dept. of Agriculture, is as near rust-proof as aparagus can be. It does fine for us; yields extraordinarily large crops and the individual shoots are large and well colored. We have 250,000 plants for sale. 1-yr. plants: 25 for 50c; 100 for $1.25; 1000 for $8.00. 2-yr. plants: 25 for $1.00; 100 for $2.00; 1000 for $15.00. 3-yr. plants: 25 for $1.25; 100 for $3.00; 1000 for $20.00. 4-yr. plants: 25 for $1.50; 100 for $3.00; 1000 for $25.00.

Mary Washington—1-yr. roots, 25 for 75c; 100 for $2.00; 1000 for $15.00.

MARTHA WASHINGTON ASPARAGUS

OTHER VARIETIES

Palmetto, Reading Giant, Colossal, Barr's Mammoth, Columbian White, Donald's Elmira, Giant Argenteuil. Price, 1-year: 25, 50c; 100, $1.25; 1000, $8.00. 2-year: 25, 75c; 100, $2.00; 1000, $12.00. 3-year: 25, $1.00; 100, $2.50; 1000, $20.00. Write for prices on large lots if you plan to make an extensive planting.

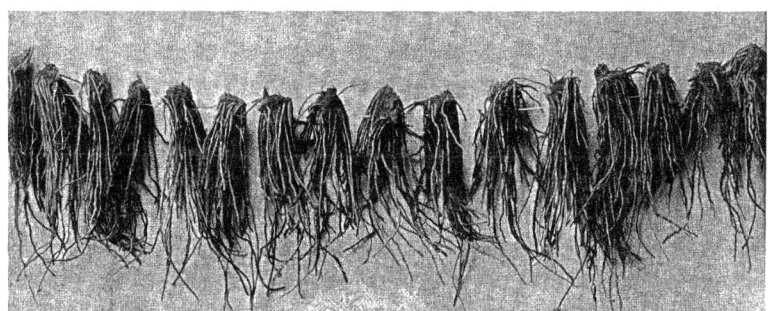

TYPICAL ROOTS OF MARTHA WASHINGTON ASPARAGUS

33

Garden Roots and Vegetable Plants

HORSERADISH ROOTS

Horseradish is in great demand in the early spring for flavoring meats, pickles and other foods. It is easy to grow in your home garden. Select a spot where the soil is rich and deep, and not likely to be plowed or disturbed for several years; for to do its best, horseradish should remain in the same place for years. Set the young roots, pointed end down, in rows 3 to 4 feet apart, with roots 1 foot apart in the row. Keep the weeds out for the first year and the horseradish will take care of itself. In digging, enough of the roots will remain in the soil to make provision for the future. For commercial field culture about 10,000 plants are required to the acre if set 1 x 4. It requires considerable skill to produce the large, fat roots that you see on the market, and we are glad to correspond with growers who plan to set a half-acre or so for market purposes. The new Bohemian variety is claimed to be far superior to the common horseradish. Prices: Maliner Kren, 75c per 25; $2.00 per 100; $15.00 per 1000.

Common Horseradish Roots—50c per 25; $1.00 per 100; $7.50 per 1000.

HORSERADISH

RHUBARB OR PIE PLANT

Rhubarb is the first vegetable to come in the early spring. If boxes or barrels are placed over them during the first few warm days, it will hasten the maturity so that you can cut the stalks a week or more earlier. If clumps are taken up with earth on the roots in the fall and allowed to freeze solid, and then placed in a dark part of the cellar, cuttings of fine rhubarb stalks can be made all through the winter. Rhubarb will grow in most any soil, but does best in a deep, rich loam which is top dressed each fall with rich manure. When the plants get old and root bound they should be replaced with new plants.

Linnaeus—A medium-sized variety with reddish stalks of fine quality. Prices: 15c each; $1.25 per 12; $8.00 per 100; $60.00 per 1000.

Victoria—A large, pale green variety, good quality, with large leaves and stalks. Late and very productive. Prices: 20c each; $1.50 per 12; $10.00 per 100.

Johnson—This is a new variety we procured from the late Edw. Johnson, horticulturist, having been perfected by him. It is the largest, most vigorous and productive, as well as the finest flavored rhubarb in cultivation. It appears to be a cross of the Linneaus and Victoria, retaining the reddish color and flavor of the Linneaus and the large size and vigor of the Victoria. The stalks are very large, tender and of delicate flavor. We have a very large stock and have reduced the price. 25c each; $2.00 per 10; $15.00 per 100; $125.00 per 1000. Selected, extra size roots, 35c each; $3.00 per 10; $20.00 per 100.

Rhubarb for Forcing—Extra large roots, 4 and 5 years old, for forcing in winter, 50% additional to the prices above.

VEGETABLE PLANTS

Our Frost-Proof Cabbage Plants can be set 4 to 6 Weeks Earlier than Home Grown Plants, and will Mature Heads 2 to 3 Weeks Earlier.

These plants are grown for us in South Carolina and Georgia, where conditions are ideal for the growth of hard, tough plants in the open field. We can fill orders from December 1st to May 1st.

Varieties: Early Jersey Wakefield, Charleston Wakefield, Copenhagen Market, Golden Acre, Succession and Early Flat Dutch.

Prices: By mail, postage paid, lots of 100 and 200 plants at 75c per 100 plants; 500 plants for $2.25; 1000 plants for $4.00.

By express, buyer paying express charges: 1000 to 4000 at $2.50 per 1000; 5000 and over $2.00 per 1000. Express shipments are packed 1000 and 2000 to the package and weigh about 20 lbs. to the 1000.

FROST-PROOF ONION PLANTS

Our Frost-Proof Onion Plants are just as hardy as the Frost-Proof Cabbage plants. We offer the two most popular varieties: White Bermuda and Yellow Bermuda. Prices on Onion Plants same as Cabbage Plants.

HOLT'S MAMMOTH SAGE

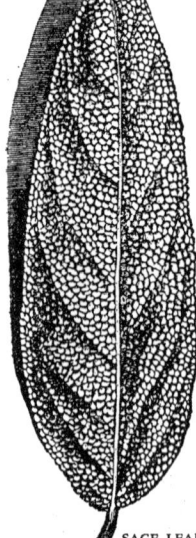

Holt's Mammoth is different from the common sage, in that it never produces seeds, but multiplies by root divisions. Plants grow a foot or more in height and 3 feet in diameter. The leaves are large and thick, and produced in enormous quantities. Culture: Set the plants in deep, rich soil about 1½ x 3 feet apart. Maintain thorough cultivation. If the plants are left in the same place from year to year, it is well to cut off the old tops each spring and encourage new growth. When they have attained full size the leaves should be picked by hand and spread thinly and evenly in a cool, airy place to dry; then they made be stored in heavy paper sacks. We supply the local market with sage leaves of our own growing.

Sage Roots (Holt's Mammoth)—25c each; $1.50 per 10; $2.25 per 25; $6.00 per 100; $50.00 per 1000.

SAGE LEAF   Dried Sage Leaves for flavoring, etc., 1 oz., 15c; ¼ lb., 35c; 1 lb., $1.00.

34

a great deal more profitable than a bumper crop, when the markets are flooded.

Garden Roots and Vegetable Plants

SOME FROST-PROOF CABBAGE PLANTS

HOME GROWN CABBAGE PLANTS

Ready in May, June and July. Varieties: Golden Acre, Copenhagen Market, Danish Ball Head, Succession, Wakefield, Surehead, Late Drumhead, Fottlers Brunswick, Mammoth Rock, Red, Winningstadt, etc. 50c per 100; $3.00 per 1000; $20.00 per 10,000. If in need of a large quantity of cabbage or other plants, correspond with us for prices.

TOMATO PLANTS

Field Grown Plants—Ready in May and June. Varieties: Earliana, Stones, John Bear, Greater Baltimore, Bonny Best, Dwarf Champion, Matchless, Ponderosa, Golden Queen. Prices: 25, 50c; 100, $1.25; 1000, $5.00.
Greenhouse Grown—25, 75c; 100, $2.50; 1000, $20.00.

SWEET POTATO PLANTS

Ready in May, June and July. Varieties: Jersey Red and Yellow, Vineland Bush, Red Bermuda, Jersey Big Stem Improved. Prices: 25, 50c; 100, $1.50; 1000, $8.00.

CELERY PLANTS

Ready in May, June, July and August. Varieties: White Plume, Golden Self Blanching, Dwarf Golden Heart, Giant Pascal. Prices, Field Grown, 25, 35c; 100, 75c; 1000, $3.50. Transplanted, from flats, 25, 75c; 100, $2.00; 1000, $12.00.
We make a specialty of the Golden Self Blanching Celery, and can quote low prices in large lots of plants.

CAULIFLOWER PLANTS

Ready in May, June and July. Varieties: Early Snowball, Dwarf Erfurt, Danish Giant, Dry Weather. Prices, 25, 50c; 100, $1.00; 1000, $6.00.

PEPPER PLANTS

Ready in May and June. Varieties: Red Chili, Red Cayenne, Bull Nose, Ruby King, Sweet Mountain. Prices, 25, 75c; 100, $2.00; 1000, $15.00.

EGG PLANTS

Ready in May and June. Varieties: New York Improved, Black Beauty. Prices, 25, 75c; 100, $2.50; 1000, $20.00.

MISCELLANEOUS VEGETABLE PLANTS

Lettuce, Beets, Brussels Sprouts, Kale, Kohl Rabi and Parsley. 25, 35c; 100, 75c; 1000, $3.50.

SEED POTATOES

Axtell's Early—A new potato of the Cobbler type. It is white, of the very best flavor, nearly round, with deep eyes, the sure sign of quality. Earlier and more productive than Cobbler, we think the best early potato we know. Some potatoes are good one year and poor the next; Axtell's Early is always a fine eating potato. 1 lb., 25c; pk., $1.00; bu., $3.50.
Irish Cobbler—This is the round white potato so much grown in the South for the early Northern markets. 1 lb., 15c; 1 pk., 75c; bu., $2.50.
Rural Russett—A late potato with a russety skin, large, oval, smooth, enormously productive. 1 lb., 15c; pk., 75c; bu., $2.50.
Green Mountain—A fine quality potato, largely grown in many sections for late market.
Sir Walter Raleigh—An oblong, late variety popular in some sections. Very productive, fine quality.
Bugless—A late red potato of very fine quality, very productive and so vigorous a grower that the bugs have no effect on the foliage. If you plant Bugless, you are sure of potatoes every year.
Dooley — Large, round, medium early, white.
Woodruff — One week later than Cobbler, oblong, white, fine quality, valuable.
Early Rose—The old standby; price same as Cobbler.
Following varieties, same price as Russett.

SEED
POTATOES

AXTELL'S EARLY
POTATOES

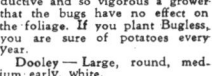

35

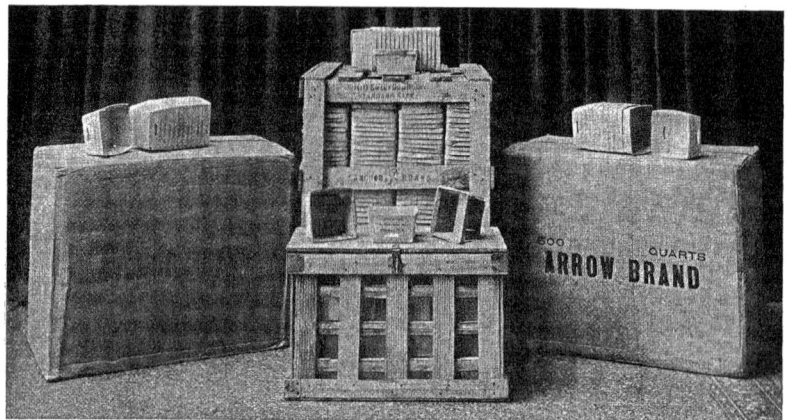

Berry Baskets

WE offer the "Arrow" and "Anchor" brand of baskets, made in Virginia. The Arrow brand come from the outside of the log and are all nice and white. The Anchor brand is made just the same, but is the "run of the log," some being a little discolored. These baskets are made of nice white wood, cut heavy, and are not to be compared with ordinary baskets. They will not bulge out and "weewaw" when filled with fruit. They are the firmest and most substantial of any berry basket we have ever seen and no fruit grower, who has once used them, will use any other if he can get these brands. They weigh, when crated, 125 pounds to the 1000 baskets, whereas, ordinary baskets weigh but 85 pounds to the 1000. They cost a little more, but are more economical to use than cheaper baskets, as they hold the fruit firm and it does not settle in the basket, like in other makes.

SOMETHING NEW IN THE BERRY BASKET LINE

This year, we offer "Arrow" and "Anchor" brand berry baskets in heavy pasteboard cartons, holding 500 baskets each. These will be very convenient to handle and where one wants but 500 baskets, he will not have to purchase a full thousand in order to get the benefit of the 1000 rate. 500 baskets, in carton, weigh 50 pounds.

PRICES OF BERRY BASKETS, 1929

Arrow Brand Quarts, $1.25 per 100; 500, $5.00; 1000, $10.00.

Anchor Brand Quarts and Pints—$1.20 per 100; 500, $4.75; 1000, $9.50.

New York State Made Baskets — $1.00 per 100, $8.00 per 1000.

New Beaverboard Baskets — 100, $1.50; 1000, $11.00. With trade name and business phrase or slogan, printed on each basket, $1.00 per 1000, extra.

Special—We will allow a discount of 50c per 1000 on all orders for baskets received before April 1st.

QUART BASKET

PRICES OF BERRY CRATES

We handle the standard 32 quart or bushel berry crate. It is substantial and well made, having four layers of 8 quarts each, with 3 separators. Price 65c, $6.00 per 10.

Smaller Crates—Crates holding 8 quarts or 12 pints, with seperators, 35c each; $3.00 per 10. Crates holding 16 quarts or 24 pints, 45c each, $4.00 per 10.

HOTKAPS

The New Method of Plant Protection

These caps or "Kaps" are about a foot in diameter, made of almost transparent paper and when placed over young plants, or hills of melons, cucumbers, etc., protect the plants from the frosts and excessive rains and hasten the maturity of the plants. In order to adjust them properly, it is necessary to have the Hot Kap Setters, which enables one to place the "Kap" in such a position on the ground, that it will be almost air tight and not collapsible. These Hot Kaps are extensively used in California and other places where early vegetable crops are largely grown. We will be glad to send circulars and full particulars to anyone interested. Price of Hot Kaps, 250 trial package and 1 special type garden setter, $4.00. 1000 lots, $11.50; 5000, $55.00; 10,000, $107.50. Germaco Steel Hot Kap Setter, $2.50.

36

Farmer's Baby Chicks

Our baby chick business has increased each year for several years. You absolutely run no risk in sending to us for baby chicks. The flocks from which the eggs are gathered for producing these chicks are the very best to be had, culled and inspected by state authorities. We do not advise ordering chicks to come much before warm weather sets in, unless you have special facilities for caring for them.

OUR GUARANTEE TO YOU

We guarantee to deliver chicks to you in first-class condition. On arrival of chicks, open the carton or box in the presence of the post-man or express agent, and have them mark the number on the back of the receipt, if there be any dead. Send this receipt to us and we will refund your money for the dead ones or send you enough more to make you good. If it is only a few, we prefer to return the money.

PRICES OF BABY CHICKS FOR 1929

Prices in the following table are for chicks shipped out in April, May and early June. If shipped in February or March, add 20% or 1-5, to these prices. If ordered for late June or July shipment, deduct 10% or 1-10, from these prices. We can supply baby chicks in any quantity and will be pleased to correspond with large prospective buyers. At these prices, chicks are sent postpaid to any part of the United States, when cash in full accompanies the order, or is sent before shipment is made. If we send C. O. D. for part of the cost of the chicks, the postage is also included in the C. O. D.

	25	50	100
Single Comb White Leghorns	$5.00	$ 8.00	$14.00
Single Comb Brown Leghorns	5.00	8.00	14.00
Single Comb Buff Leghorns	5.00	8.00	14.00
Single Combed Anconas	6.00	9.00	16.00
Barred Plymouth Rocks	6.00	9.00	16.00
S. C. Rhode Island Reds	6.00	9.00	16.00
S. C. Black Minorcas	7.00	10.00	18.00
White Minorcas	7.00	10.00	18.00
Buff Plymouth Rocks	7.00	10.00	18.00
White Plymouth Rocks	7.00	10.00	18.00
White Wyandottes	7.00	10.00	18.00
Buff Orpingtons	7.00	10.00	18.00
Black Langshans	7.00	10.00	18.00
White Langshans	7.00	10.00	18.00
Light Brahmas	7.00	11.00	20.00
White Orpingtons	7.00	10.00	18.00
Silver Laced Wyandottes	7.00	10.00	18.00
Left Overs (Heavy Mixed Kinds)	5.00	8.00	14.00
Left Overs (Light Mixed Kinds)	4.00	7.00	13.00

Pekin Duck Eggs—$1.50 per 11. Ducklings, 35c each; 25 for $7.50.

R. I. Red Eggs (Best Matings)—$1.50 per 15; $2.50 per 30; $7.00 per 100.

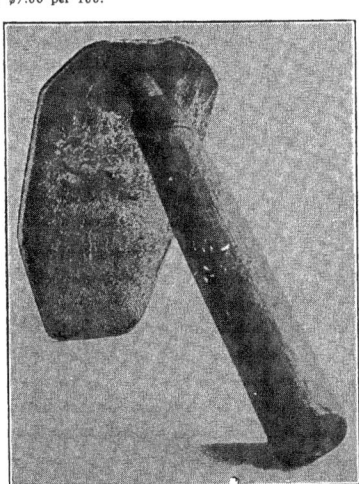

FARMER'S TALLY SYSTEM

For Keeping Tally with Berry Pickers, Hop Pickers

This consists of cards printed with four rows of checked off spaces, each space representing a certain number of quarts. On one side of the card are the "1-qt." spaces and on the other the "4-qt." spaces. Near the eye-hole is a space for writing the name of the picker. The proprietor's name can be written on the back. There are 100 cards furnished with each outfit and an up-to-date railroad conductor's punch. When the pickers go to the field, they take one of these cards with a string through the eye-hole and put the string about their neck. When they have picked a "handy," or four quart pick-ing stand full of berries, the man who has charge of them takes it from them and punches out a space in the card to represent the number of quarts picked. There are 20 "4-qt." spaces and 20 "1-qt." spaces, so when the spaces are all punched out, the picker has picked 100 quarts. Price of complete tally system, punch and 100 cards, $3.00, postpaid. Extra cards, 50c per 100.

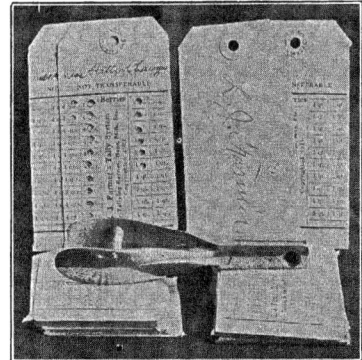

FARMER'S HANDY STRAWBERRY SETTER

For Setting Strawberry, Raspberry, Tomato, Cabbage and Other Plants

This tool is so simple, it requires no skill to operate it. Any-one can set strawberry or vegetable plants with Farmer's Straw-berry Setter, as it has no complicated mechanism and sets plants more easily and in better shape than any other tool made. It consists of a blade about 3-16 inch thick, 3 to 4 inches wide and about 8 inches long, with a handle inserted at right angles with the blade, very similar in shape to an adz. These tools are hand forged, made of the very best material by a local blacksmith, and will last a lifetime if properly cared for. Not only is this tool the very best thing ever devised for setting strawberry plants, but it is also fine for working among the runners, and for heeling in, or rather tipping in black raspberry plants. Price, $1.50 each; $5.00 per 4. Your money back if not satisfied.

porches and other places where wanted. The leaves and vine are pretty, being ovate or V shaped. It seems to be the most popular comparatively cheap vine an find. Pieces of tubers will grow, like cut potatoes. It is supposed to winter most localities, but we recommend planting only in well drained places and put-ch over the roots to protect from the coldest weather of winter. The demand ubers has been enormous during the past few years and we have only just caught he demand. We have now a plentiful supply. When growing, the vine re-at of the sweet potato.

PRICES OF CINNAMON TUBERS

1 size—4 to 6 inches long, 10c each; 3 for 25c; 7 for 50c; 15 for $1.00; 100,

Tubers—2 years old, 6 to 10 inches, 20c each; 3 for 50c; 7 for $1.00; 15 for 0 for $12.00.

Tubers—3 years old, 10 to 15 inches long, 30c each; 3 for 75c; 7 for $1.50; 15 ; 100 for $15.00.

E PLANTS—If you are interested in Geraniums, Begonias, House Ferns, Hy-Carnations, Chrysanthemums, Fuchsias and other inside plants, send for our list, which is omitted from this catalog on account of space.

ANNUAL FLOWERING PLANTS

n supply Greenhouse Grown Asters, Marigolds, Zinnias, Snap Dragons, Ten ocks, and similar plants at 50c per 10; $3.50 per 100. Salvias, Coleus, Petunias, etc., 75c per 10; $5.00 per 100. Field Grown Aster plants, ready in June and per 10; $1.25 per 100; $6.00 per 1000.

ES
a, Easter and 20 other
ite for list and prices.

I SPAWN
Spawn—Per brick, 30c; 5
freight. 10 bricks, $2.00;
s, $17.00.

OWERING BULBS
per 10; $2.50 per 100;

; $3.50 to $5.00 per 100.
per 10; $6.00 to $15.00

.00 per 100.
:h; $1.75 per 10; $10.00

and special prices.

IN SEASON
icked strawberries, rasp-
its, gooseberries, grapes,
ies, peaches and quinces.
antity wanted.

TY, NEW YORK
            May 31st, 1928
e condition and we think you
them in the baskets so they
a your stock.
RS. G. M. SCHUYLER.

, NORTH CAROLINA
        April 4th, 1928
u an order and were so well
e have intended ordering more
d will leave it to you to send
    MRS. O. J. HOLLER.

THE STRYON PICKET FENCE

Comes in rolls of 50, 75 and 100 feet.

Heavy—3 feet high, 2 inches between pickets. Pickets 2 x 5-8 inches, 4 cables; 12½ wire, 12c per foot. 4 feet high, 2 inches between pickets. Pickets 2 x 5-8 inches, 5 cables; 12½ wire, 16c per foot. 5 feet high, 2 inches between pickets. Pickets 2 x 5-8 inches, 6 cables; 12½ wire, 20c per foot.

Light—3 feet high, 2 inches between pickets. Pickets 2 x 3-8 inches, 4 cables; 12½ wire, 9c per foot. 4 feet high, 2 inches between pickets. Pickets 2 x 3-8 inches, 5 cables; 12½ wire, 12c per foot.

Peat Moss—$4.00 per bale.

CLINTARK PLASTIC TREE COMPOUND

A natural tree salve, an antiseptic plastic preparation quickly applied to protect all wounds of bark or limb. It kills and keeps out insects, fungus disease germs and prevents disfigurement, decay and death of trees. A torn or broken limb, a small patch of bark ripped off by lawn mower, plow or carelessness, may be a place for rot producing fungi to lodge, and eventually may mean the death of a valuable tree. With the use of Clintark, injuries and decay may be stopped very economically.

Write for free booklet, "How to Quickly Renew the Life of Wounded or Decayed Trees."

The cost of Clintark is only $1.25, plus a few cents postage for a 5-lb. can; 2-lb. can, 75c; 10-lb. can, $2.50, plus the postage. Full instructions for applying on each can.

PORT BURWELL, ONTARIO, CANADA
            May 10th, 1928
Received Hot Kaps in good condition, also flower seed and booklet.   CARL KLOPSFER.

home use, now before the public. We are headquarters for the trees.

The Best Hardy Perennials

BORDER PLANTING OF IRIS

GERMAN OR LIBERTY IRIS

f descriptions given, "S." refers to the Standards als, and "F." to the Falls or drooping petals.
derd—S. Yellow-bronze. F. Magenta-red. 35c;

Bluish-violet, overlaid bronze. F. Deep purple.
5c.

—S. Deep purple-violet. F. Deep velvety violet.
c.

l—Straw-yellow, with a few thin lines. 25c; 3 for

fer—S. Blue. F. Pansy-violet, with lighter edges.
c.

lainty, white Placata, brodered and suffused soft
for 60c.

Bronze, tinged with crimson. F. Maroon, veined
3 for $2.00.

Lilac-pink. F. Purplish old-rose, golden throat,
35c; 3 for 85c.

Pearl—Pale bluish-lavender, with a faint creamy
arge flowers of perfect form and exceptional sub-
creamy undertone of this exceptional substance
the luster and iridescence which we see in the
ng of sea shells which produce mother-of-pearl.
tall, a vigorous grower, and a profuse bloomer.
, far the best Iris of its color in the world. 75c;

istman—S. White, tinged violet. F. Purple, re-
e. 25c; 3 for 60c.

nearly 100 varieties of German Iris and if in-
for our complete list.

IRIS COLLECTION "A"
d Varieties, our selection, $2.00.

IRIS COLLECTION "B"
ed Varieties, our selection, of varieties
over 50c each, $4.50.

is in purple, yellow, lavender and blue colors,
.25 per 10; $8.00 per 100. In pink and white
ich; $1.50 per 10; $10.00 per 100.

JAPANESE IRIS
d—Pure white, 35c; 3 for 85c.
—Pale, pink, lavender veined.
—White, spotted purple.
ama—Violet. Blooms in clusters.
—Dark red, shaded maroon.
d—Light blue, shaded darker.
lich, velvety purple.
lilac-blue, veined, white center on each petal.
g—French-grey, veined violet.
s, 35c each; 3 for 85c; 10 for $2.50.
ese Iris—Grows to moderate height and is loaded

SINGLE AND DOUBLE HOLLYHOCKS
Allegheny Type—Very distinct, ruffled, satiny. 25c each; $2.00 per 10.
Double Hollyhocks—Colors, Black, white, yellow, pink, red. 25c each; $2.00 per 10.
Single Hollyhocks—Assorted colors, mixed. 10c each; 75c per 10; $5.00 per 100. 2-year, transplanted plants, 15c each; $1.25 per 10; $10.00 per 100. We have a fine supply of Hollyhock plants.

THE MOST POPULAR PERENNIALS
In addition to Iris, Phlox, Peonies, Hollyhocks and Sweet William, the following are the most planted and therefore the most popular perennials:
Campanula (Canterbury Bells)—25c each; $2.00 per 10; $15.00 per 100.
Delphinium (Perennial Larkspur) — Belladonna, Bellamosa and Gold Medal Hybrids. 30c each; $2.50 per 10.
Dicentra Spectabilis (Bleeding Heart)—60c each; $5.00 per 10.
Digitalis (Foxglove)—20c each; $1.75 per 10.
Oriental Poppy—25c each; $2.00 per 10.

SWEET WILLIAM (Dianthus Barbatus)
We have about 10,000 plants, all varieties and colors mixed, splendid kinds. 10c each; 10 plants, 75c; 100, $5.00. 2-year plants, 15c each; $1.25 per 10; $8.00 per 100.

OTHER PERENNIALS
Achillea (Ball of Snow)—The Pearl. 15c each; $1.25 per 10.
Anemone (Wind Flower)—Alba, Rubra and Queen Charlotte. 25c each; $2.00 per 10.
Aquilegia (Columbine)—Long Spurred. 25c each; $2.00 per 10.
Anchusa (Dropmore)—25c each; $2.00 per 10.
Aster (Hardy Daisy)—20c each; $1.75 per 10.
Bellis Perennis (Double Daisy)—15c each; $1.25 per 10.
Boltonia—15c each; $1.25 per 10.
Centaurea Montana (Cornflower)—15c each; $1.25 per 10.
Cerastium Tomentosum (Snow in Summer)—20c each; $1.75 per 10.
Phys. Franchetti (Chinese Lantern Plant)—15c each; $1.25 per 10.
Chrysanthemums—Hardy, all colors. 20c each; $1.75 per 10.
Shasta Daisy—20c each; $1.75 per 10.
Christmas Rose—75c each.
Coreopsis—15c each; $1.25 per 10.
Euphorbia Corollata (Japanese Spurge)—20c each; $1.75 per 10.
Funkia—20c each; $1.75 per 10.
Gaillardia—20c each; $1.75 per 10.
Geum—20c each; $1.75 per 10.
Gypsophila (Baby's Breath)—20c each; $1.75 per 10.
Hardy Ornamental Grasses (Japan Rush, Zebra Grass)—20c each; $1.75 per 10.
Hardy Violets—25c each; $2.00 per 10.
Helianthus (Sunflower)—15c each; $1.25 per 10.
Hemerocallis (Day Lily)—20c each; $1.50 per 10.
Hibiscus, Peachblow (Marsh Mallow)—20c each; $1.75 per 10.
Iberis Sempervirens (Candytuft)—25c each; $2.00 per 10.
Hypericum Henryii (Gold Flower)—50c each; $4.00 per 10.
Lathyrus Latifolius (Perennial Pea)—15c each; $1.25 per 10.
Blazing Star, or Gay Feather—25c each; $2.00 per 10.
Lily of the Valley—10c each; 65c per 10; $4.00 per 100.
Lupine—25c each; $2.00 per 10.
Monarda Didyma (Burgamont)—20c each; $1.75 per 10.
Forget-Me-Not—20c each; $1.75 per 10.
Giant Pansies—All colors and variations. 10c each; 60c per 10.
Iberis Sempervirens (Candytuft)—25c each; $2.00 per 10.
Myrtle (Vinca Minor)—15c each; $1.25 per 10.
Iceland Poppy—25c each; $2.00 per 10.
Hardy Scotch Pinks—White and pink. 25c each; $2.00 per 10.
Balloon Flower—20c each; $1.75 per 10.
English Primrose—25c each; $2.00 per 10.
Pyrethrum—20c each; $1.75 per 10.
Golden Glow—20c each; $1.75 per 10; $15.00 per 100.
Sedum—25c each; $2.00 per 10.
Meadow Sweet—20c each; $1.75 per 10.
Stokes' Aster—20c each; $1.75 per 10.
Red Hot Poker—30c each; $2.50 per 10.
Blue Bird Flower—20c each; $1.75 per 10.
Veronica—25c each; $2.00 per 10.

PERENNIAL PHLOX

We have a fine supply of Hardy Phlox, at least 20,000 plants of the very best colors. Note our low prices. Special prices by the 100 and 1000.

Champ de Elysees — Bright, rosy magenta, with broad flower heads. One of the very prettiest. 25c each; $2.00 per 10. 2-year clumps, 35c each; $3.00 per 10.

Eclaireur—Bright, rosy carmine. 20c each; $1.75 per 10.

F. G. Von Lassburg—Pure white, immense panicles, tall grower. 20c each; $1.75 per 10. 2-year clumps, 30c each; $2.75 per 10.

Europa—White, with crimson eye or center, very vigorous and healthy. 20c each; $1.75 per 10. 2-year clumps, 30c each; $2.75 per 10.

Iris—Light purple or lavender. 20c each; $1.75 per 10.

Lothair—Bright crimson. 20c each; $1.75 per 10.

Michael Buchner—Lavender, beautiful, tall growing and vigorous. 20c each; $1.75 per 10.

Miss Lingard — Pure white. The earliest of all, blooming a month before other varieties. 25c each; $2.00 per 10.

Mrs. Jenkins — The well-known, medium, early white, very satisfactory. 20c each; $1.75 per 10.

Rhinelander — Beautiful salmon pink. 25c each; $2.00 per 10.

Rijnstrom—Lively shade of rose-pink, very large. 20c each; $1.75 per 10.

R. P. Struthers—Cherry-red, suffused salmon. 20c each; $1.75 per 10.

Sir Edward Landseer—Bright crimson. 20c each; $1.75 per 10.

H. O. Wigers—White, with crimson center; similar to Europa, but earlier and not so tall. 20c each; $1.75 per 10.

XXX Phlox—Beautiful shade of pink. 20c each; $2.00 per 10.

Jean de Arc—25c each; $2.00 per 10.

Any of the above will be supplied in large, 2-year-old clumps at an additional price of 10c per clump; $1.00 per 10 above the regular price.

ADAMS IMPROVED ELDERBERRY

Adams Improved Elderberry

A new fruit perfected from the common elderberry of the fields. Very suitable for pies, sauce and other purposes. Everyone likes elderberries in some form, but up to the advent of this improved variety, the only way to get them was out in the fields, by the sides of fences. Here is an improved variety, the berries of which sometimes measure nearly one-third of an inch in diameter. A few bushes in the corner of your yard or garden will produce all the fruit you will need. The berries are not only larger, but finer in every way than the wild variety. Prices: Single plants 40c; $3.50 per 10; $30.00 per 100. (Grown from seeds.) Extra selected large strain, grown from cuttings, 60c each; $5.00 per 10.

HAND-MADE MARKET BASKETS

We can supply hand-made market baskets, made by an old basket maker, at 70c for 1-peck size; 80c for 2-peck or half-bushel size; and $1.00 for 3-peck size. These are made strong and durable, just as they used to make them years ago when our fathers and mothers were here. They are made of white ash split splints, the old way, and are not to be compared with the cheap baskets usually offered in these days. They will last a lifetime and are very handy in sending eggs and other produce to market.

MRS. FLYNN'S KNEE CUSHIONS

For scrubbing, painting, dusting, gardening and other work. Invaluable to the person who has to work on his knees. $1.50 per pair.

40

S (Campanula Medium)
tion, Page 40)

PHLOX (Champs d' Elysees)
(See Description, Page 40)

((Europa)
tion, Page 40)

DELPHINIUM (Gold Medal Hybrids)
(See Description, Page 40)

'MASS PLANTING OF PEONIES

PEONIES

THE following list of Peonies will be found to be most satisfactory. They have been selected after consultation with the best authorities on peonies in the United States. If in want of other varieties of peonies, send for our most complete list of Up-to-Date Peonies; we have not room to list them all here. The figures after each name of variety, represents the rating given them by the American Peony Society, on a basis of 10 for perfect. Thus, Albert Crousse is rated 8.6. Our peony roots are carefully dug and the roots carefully pruned and shortened, ready for planting. We offer only strong divisions with 3 to 5 eyes, cut from mature plants, the best to be had.

FOUR GOOD PEONIES

The following four make a worthy collection which should have a place in every garden. We recommend ordering them, if you can afford but 4 good peonies. At catalog prices they amount to $4.00. We will supply them for $3.00.

Festiva Maxima (white), Edulis Superba (mauve-pink), Monsieur Jules Elie (rose-pink) and Felix Crousse (ruby-red).

PEONIES ACCORDING TO COLOR

We will supply good strong divisions of desirable peonies, not named, at following prices. White Varieties 35c each, 3 for $1.00. Pink Varieties 30c each, 4 for $1.00. Red Varieties 60c each, 3 for $1.50. One each, white, pink and red, $1.20. Special prices on 100 and 1000 lots.

THE THREE VERY BEST PEONIES

Regardless of price, the best three peonies are LeCygne, Solange and Therese. We will send one large division of each for $12.00. Regular price, $14.00.

WHITE VARIETIES

Avalanche 8.7—Large, globular, snow-white, with collar of creamy-white. Center tinted lilac-white, with some petals edged carmine. Tall, strong, upright grower, free bloomer. Late midseason. $1.00 each.

Baroness Schroeder 9.0—Globular. Opens delicate flesh-white, changing to creamy-white. Rose fragrance. Strong, upright grower. Late midseason. $1.50.

Couronne D'Or 8.1—Pure white, with bright yellow stamens and carmine tips on a few of the center petals. Splendid grower, late midseason. Semi-rose form. 75c.

Duchesse D'Nemours 8.1—Crown type. Clear white, with collar of sulphur-white and greenish marble at the center. Medium height, vigorous grower. Early. Fragrant. 50c.

Festiva Maxima 9.3—Most popular white variety. 75c.

Marie Jacquin 8.3—Delicate flesh tint, changing to lilac-white. Semi-double flower, but often single on young plants. Strong grower, free bloomer. Globular. Midseason, very interesting. $1.50.

Marie Lemoine 8.5—Pure white, shading to creamy-white in the center, with slight carmine markings on some petals. Fragrant. Rose form. Dwarf plant with strong stems. Very late. $1.00.

James Kelway 8.7 — Opens dainty flesh-pink, changing to flesh-white. Flowers immense, semi-rose type. Plant vigorous, doing best on clay soils. $1.50.

LeCygne 9.9—Perfect rose type. Color creamy-white, with a greenish luminosity at the heart changing to pure white. Often called, "The Swan." Fragrant, midseason. Voted the nearest perfect peony by American Peony Society. Ea. $7.50.

Solange, 9.7—Perfect rose type. Deep canary-white, shaded orange-salmon at the heart and suffused with a hue of reddish-brown, suggesting the "Tea Shade" of the millinery trade. Vigorous, tall, strong, late. Rivals LeCygne for first place. $3.50.

PINK VARIETIES OF PEONIES

Edulis Superba 7.6—Mauve-pink; fragrant and early. 75c.

Albert Crousse 8.6 — Soft shell-pink. Ball-shaped, large blooms. Tall, erect. Late. $1.00.

Eugenie Verdier 8.6—Hydrangea-pink, outer petals lighter, with center deeper, lightly flecked crimson. Fragrant and fine for cut flowers. Crown type. $1.00.

Livingstone 8.1—Imbricated petals, pale lilac-rose, silvery tipped; center petals flecked with carmine. Rose type, strong grower, late. $1.00.

Marguerite Gerard 8.4—Semi-rose. Pale, hydrangea-pink, changing to creamy-white; center petals minutely flecked dark carmine. Strong grower, free bloomer. Late, midseason. $1.00.

Mons. Jules Elie 9.2 — Largest and most striking pink. $1.50.

Sarah Bernhardt 9.0—Semi-rose type. Mauve-rose, tipped silver; delightfully fragrant; strong, vigorous, late midseason. $2.00.

Therese 9.8—Full rose type. Light violet-rose, shading to lilac-white at the center. Fragrant, midseason. One of the three greatest. $3.00.

Lady Alexander Duff 9.1—Semi-rose form. Opens soft flesh-pink, changing to French-white, suffused blush; making the flower neither true white nor pink. Upright, vigorous grower, midseason. $3.00.

Mme. Emile Galle 8.5—Translucent lilac-white with an opalescent shading of shell-pink, changing to milk-white in the center. Strong grower, medium tall, free bloomer. Late mid-season. Rose type. $1.00.

Reine Hortense 8.7—Semi-rose type. Uniform hydrangea-pink with the color minutely flecked on a white ground and guards and center petals marked carmine, slightly fragrant. Tall, medium strong. Midseason. $1.50.

Claire DuBois 8.7—Globular type. Clear, violet-rose, tipped silvery-white. Medium tall, erect, late. $1.00.

RED VARIETIES OF PEONIES

Benjamin Franklin 8.1—Semi-rose. Brilliant crimson, shaded dark er at the base of petals. Tall, erect, early midseason. $1.00. k

Felix Crousse 8.4—The best red for cut flowers. $1.00.

Karl Rosenfield 8.8—Best all-round red peony. Semi-rose type. Velvety crimson. Vigorous grower, midseason. $1.00.

Longfellow 9.0—Semi-rose form. Brightest crimson, with cherry tone and without the violet hues which are so objectionable to many; the most brilliant red peony. Good grower, late midseason. $1.00.

Richard Carvel 8.8 — Bomb type. Earliest of the reds to bloom. Uniform bright crimson. Fragrant, good grower. $3.00.

M. Martin Cahuzac 8.8—Semi-rose type. Dark purple-garnet, with a black reflex and golden stamens. Midseason, good grower. The darkest good peony. $2.50.

42

Dahlias

nd October and is
They are as easily
t the same culture.
noisture and this is
e fall season is wet.
g six kinds, and have
ne can afford to have
atly admired by every-

$1.75 per 10; $3.00

25c each; $2.00 per

iowy. Price, see white.
beautiful, velvety, dark

Price, see yellow.
ow. Price, see yellow.
ive 6 varieties, amount-
of the 6 varieties, for
or $7.00.
:s, mixed. 10c each;

IAL MERIT
profuse bloomer, extra
in cut. 50c.
eation. Flowers of very
inging to a soft, rosy
I on long, stiff
er variety. 50c.
ne of the best.

ker than rhoda-
e. The flower

t cactus Dahlia
ely blending to

m dark to pink-
od stems. 50c.
i pink. 25c.

on good stems.
ite in a streaked
with petals in-
eld in a manner
$2.00.
A clear, light
flower. $2.00.
ng to lemon in

shadings. 25c.

IAS
yellow. 25c.
meo-pink. 25c.
of one of the
lentical with the
an improvement
I in form. 50c.
iuff and yellow.
produced freely

pointed at tips.
iodamine-purple.

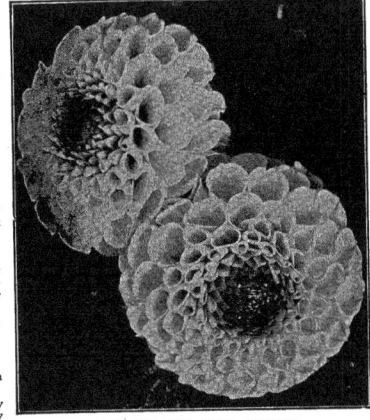

WHITE DAHLIAS (SHOW)

Bonnie Brae (Dec.)—This is one of the best Dahlias ever grown. The color of this wonderful Dahlia is a peach and cream combination of shadings, showing strong on the peach-pink at first, but after well opened comes out much lighter. The flowers this season grew from 8 to 10 inches in diameter and were carried on stems from 18 inches to 2 feet long. Very free flowering. $1.00 each.

Eleanor Grant (Dec.)—Large flowers borne on extra long stems, the outer petals of light cameo-pink, while the center is sea foam green. A fine Dahlia. $1.00.

Junior—An enormous flower, one of the largest Dahlias grown. A pure lavender. Fine for exhibition purposes. $1.00.

Mrs. Carl Salbach—A sensational Decorative Dahlia of great size. In color, a mauve-pink, with occasional blendings of white; the general impression being pink. For exhibition purposes this new creation is very desirable. $1.00.

Mrs. I. De Ver Warner—Deep mauve-pink. One of the best Dahlias. Long, stiff stems, excellent for cut flowers. $1.00.

Pride of California—Called the "American Beauty" Dahlia. Winner of Gold and Silver Medals. Huge crimson-red flowers produced on long, straight stems. $1.00.

Rosa Nell—The color is a clear, bright rose, and the flowers are very large, and is one of the best shaped Decorative Dahlias grown. Good stems and habits. 50c.

Snowdrift—A giant, clear white. Flower has good depth with broad, waxy petals of the true Decorative type. $1.00.

Swift—Lemon-yellow tipped white. 50c.

The Grizzly—A prize-winning California Dahlia. A dark maroon-red, with stems 3 feet long. The flowers are large with reflexed petals and stand well above the foliage, making a fine effect in the garden. $1.00.

Wm. H. Slocombe—The largest and best pale yellow Decorative to my knowledge. A clear sulphur-yellow passing to martinus-yellow at tips. Flowers o gigantic size, from 6 to 8 inches in diameter under ordinary conditions. $1.00.

SWEET WILLIAM (Dianthus)
(See Description, Page 39)

The Beautiful Gladioli

WE consider the gladiolus the most popular flower of the day. As a cut-flower and for funeral work they are unsurpassed. If cut when the first flower on the spike opens, they will continue to bloom right out to the tip end and last a week or more, and be even more beautiful. If set early, some of the earliest kinds will bloom in a few weeks; and if set late, the last spikes of the late varieties will be hardly out of the way when hard freezes come. Beautify your home and plant at least a dozen gladiolus bulbs. Our bulbs are plump and healthy.

WELL KNOWN GLADIOLUS

America, Byron L. Smith, Chris, Evelyn Kirtland, Mrs. Francis King, Gretchen Zang, Halley, Herada, Le Marechal Foch, Lily White, Mrs. Dr. Norton, Loveliness, Netherland, Niagara, Panama, Prince of Wales, Peace, Schwaben, Wilbrink, Mrs. Frank Pendleton, White Light, Early Sunrise. Prices: ½ to 1-inch bulbs, 5c each; 40c per 10; $3.00 per 100; $20.00 per 1000. 1 to 1½-inch, 8c each; 60c per 10; $4.00 per 100; $30.00 per 1000. 1½ to 2½-inch, 10c each; 75c per 10; $5.00 per 100; $40.00 per 1000.

COMPARATIVELY NEW GLADIOLUS

Challenger, Colleen, Honey Boy, Jasper, Milady, Opalescent, Parader, Priority, Remembrance, 1910 Rose, Twilight, Tyrian Beauty, Vanity. Prices: ½ to 1-inch bulbs, 10c each; 90c per 10. 1 to 1½-inch, 15c each; $1.25 per 10. 1½ to 2½-inch, 20c each; $1.50 per 10.

OUR MOST UP-TO-DATE GLADIOLUS

We had no idea there were such pretty gladiolus as the following. We don't believe they can be beaten anywhere.

Anthony Zonker—Extra tall, strong plant, with 5 to 7 blooms open at a time. Deep salmon-rose, with lower petals beautifully blotched like Pendleton. 15c each; $1.25 per 10.

Avalon—Choice blush white, beautiful throat, ruffled. 15c each; $1.25 per 10.

Big Black—Extra large, pure, rich deep red, distinct and showy, best dark red. 25c each; $2.25 per 10.

Blue Isle—Medium size, light violet-blue. 20c each; $1.75 per 10.

Buckeye—Massive flowers, fine rose-pink, with tint of old-rose at edges. Petals ruffled. 15c each; $1.25 per 10.

Bumble Bee—Large, purest salmon-rose pink. Ground penciled blue, throat deeper color. 15c each; $1.25 per 10.

Dr. J. H. Neeley—Tall grower, finest blush white, throat white, tinted light canary-yellow. 15c each; $1.80 per 10.

Fairest White—Pure white, soft pink throat. 20c each; $1.80 per 10.

Flaming Vale—Tall. Long spikes, with deep, cardinal-red flowers, throat deeper red. 20c each; $1.80 per 10.

Giant Fawn—Large, deep fawn yellow, faint blush-pink border, beautiful red line in throat. Wonderful. 15c each; $1.25 per 10.

Goshen—Deep silvery-rose-pink, showy rose-red blotches. 15c each; $1.25 per 10.

Indian Maid—Beautiful peach-blossom pink, with deeper throat. Very choice, distinct. 35c each; $3.00 per 10.

John T. Pirie—Exceptionally colored, very attractive. Mahogany-brown with yellow bordered, dark mahogany-brown throat. Very late and distinct. 25c each; $2.25 per 10.

Kasson—Large, lavender-rose pink, deeper throat. Finely ruffled. 15c each; $1.25 per 10.

Lilac Old Rose—As its name implies, a beautiful lilac-rose. Unsurpassed. 15c each; $1.25 per 10.

Mrs. Arthur Meeker—Rich, deep American Beauty rose color. Very beautiful. 15c each; $1.25 per 10.

Mrs. Geo. W. Moulton—25c each; $2.00 per 10.

44

FLAMING VALE
(See Description Opposite)

The Beautiful Gladioli

Peep-o-Day—Tall, beautiful blush pink on white ground. Grand. 15c each; $1.25 per 10.

Purple Spot—Large, violet-red, with conspicuous dark blotches. Early, showy. 15c each; $1.25 per 10.

Romance—Large, orange-salmon-rose, yellow and red throat. Petals bordered blue, distinct. 20c each; $1.80 per 10.

Rosalind—One of the most beautiful dark red gladiolus extant. Very early and attractive. 15c each; $1.25 per 10.

Rose Glow—Ruffled, purest rose-pink, deeper in throat. 15c each; $1.25 per 10.

Red Cloud—Bright red, many flowers open at a time. White bar in lower petals. Grand and much talked about. 20c each; $1.80 per 10.

Red Copper—Deep salmon-rose, heavily flaked blue; lower petals red, white and yellow, lined and penciled with blue. Attracts great attention. 20c each; $1.80 per 10.

Ruth Huntington — Beautiful violet-lilac, deeper lilac markings on lower petals. Large, tall, with fine spikes, great favorite, ruffled petals. 15c each; $1.25 per 10.

Salmon-Buff—Beautiful salmon-buff. Throat beautifully penciled yellow. 15c each; $1.25 per 10.

Salmon Plume—Clear salmon-flesh, petals edged deeper, red throat. Ruffled. 15c each; $1.25 per 10.

Senator Knox—Tall plants, large flowers, very late. White, blushed pink. 15c each; $1.25 per 10.

Shell-Pink—Rose-pink with slightly motted white throat. Tall, winner of many awards. 12c each; $1.00 per 10.

Snow Boy — Pure white, tall and stately. Large flowers, sometimes blotched on lower petals. 15c each; $1.25 per 10.

Splendora—Fine, rich, distinct dark wine-red. Splendid. 15c each; $1.25 per 10.

Thistle—Large, red-rose flower, large, pansy-like throat markings. Tall, stately. 15c each; $1.25 per 10.

DAHLIA (Decorative)

Ulysses—Large, smoky blue on rose-pink ground, deeper throat. 15c each; $1.25 per 10.

Violet Beauty — Cerise-violet, red throat blotches. Tall, large, unusual. 15c each; $1.25 per 10.

Virginia Hale—Soft, creamy salmon-rose, border of petals deeper. 15c each; $1.25 per 10.

White Pigeon—Wonderful, pure white, very large blooms, 6 to 8 open at a time. Strong, healthy, very early. 35c each; $3.00 per 10.

Youell's Favorite — Striking rosy lavender-pink. Conspicuous. 20c each; $1.80 per 10.

All varieties will be supplied in sizes 1 to 1½ inches at prices attached. If any special variety is wanted, write for prices, stating the particular kinds desired.

Miscellaneous Articles

IMPROVED BIRD NEPONSET
Waterproof Paper Flower Pot

The improved Bird Neponset Waterproof Pot is lined with a water resisting substance which enables one to grow seedlings that require to be 6 to 8 months in the pots. These pots will last over twice as long as the old Neponset paper pot. The price has not been advanced.

They take the place of Earthen Pots, at less than half price, and in most cases are just as good.

2¼ inch	100, $0.70	1000, $ 4.20	
2½ inch	100, .80	1000, 4.65	
3 inch	100, 1.00	1000, 5.95	
3½ inch	100, 1.10	1000, 7.45	
4 inch	100, 1.50	1000, 9.20	
5 inch	100, 2.00	1000, 14.25	
6 inch	100, 3.00	1000, 19.10	

500 at one-half price of 1000, plus 25c for recrating.

Advantages of Neponset paper pots over Earthern Pots:
1. They save all losses from breakage. 2. Weigh just one-tenth as much. Easier to handle. Reduce freight and express bills. 3. Hold moisture better. 4. Much less expensive. They are made of a tough, lasting and thoroughly waterproof paper. The pots may be used over and over again. Can be used in every way that earthen pots can be used. Ideal for transplanting and shipping potted plants and for rooting or shipping strawberry, tomato or cabbage plants. Sample mailed for 5 cents.

SOIL DISINFECTANTS

Dipdust (for dusting seeds) — 4 oz., 50c; 1 lb., $1.75; 5 lbs., $8.00.

Uspulum (soil drench)—2 oz., 50c; 1 lb., $2.75; 5 lbs., $13.00.

Zelio Paste—Destroys rodents. 2 oz., 50c; 8 oz., $1.50; 1 lb., $2.25.

Zelio Wheat—Destroys mice, squirrels, gophers, etc., 1 oz., 35c; 1 lb., $2.00.

INOCULENTS

Humogerm—For Clover, Alfalfa, etc. ¼ bu. size, 35c; ½ bu. size, 60c; 1 bu. size, $1.00; 2½ bu. size, $2.25.

Humogerm for Beans, Peas, Cow Peas, Soy Beans, ½ bu. size, 35c; 1 bu. size, 60c; 5 bu. size, $2.25.

Humogerm, garden size, for Peas, Beans and Sweet Peas, 25c.

Farmogerm (Jelly) — Same size, same price as Humogerm.

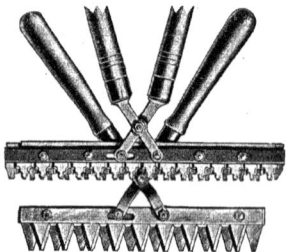

SIMPLICITY TRIMMERS AND PRUNERS

Simplicity Hedge Trimmer (upper tool in illustration), $4.00 each.
Simplicity Hedge Pruner and Trimmer (lower tool), $6.00 each.

Bird's IMPROVED NEPONSET Flower Pots

2¼"	2½"	3"	3½"	4"	5"	6"

FERTILIZERS FOR ALL CROPS

	Analysis	Price		
Super-Truck Garden	5-10-5	125 lb. bag $3.00	1 ton $44.75
Market Garden	4-8-7	125 lb. bag 2.75	1 ton 42.00
Iroquois Brand	4-12-4	125 lb. bag 2.80	1 ton 42.20
Continental Brand	4-8-4	125 lb. bag 2.60	1 ton 38.80
Potato Manure	3-10-6	125 lb. bag 2.70	1 ton 39.35
Animal Brand	3-8-4	125 lb. bag 2.50	1 ton 35.55
Syracuse Special	2-8-10	125 lb. bag 2.65	1 ton 38.50
Seneca Brand	2-12-2	125 lb. bag 2.40	1 ton 33.50
Indian Brand	2-8-5	125 lb. bag 2.40	1 ton 33.35
Onondaga Brand	1-9-4	125 lb. bag 2.25	1 ton 30.20
Gypsy Brand	0-10-10	125 lb. bag 2.45	1 ton 33.65
Acid Phosphate	0-16-0	125 lb. bag 1.75	1 ton 23.15

Sheep Manure (Dried and Ground Fine)—5 lbs., 40c; 10 lbs., 75c; 25 lbs., $1.25; 50 lbs., $2.00; 100 lbs., $3.25; 500 lbs., $14.00; 1000 lbs., $26.50; 1 ton, $50.00.

Bone Meal—3 lbs., 25; 5 lbs., 40c; 10 lbs., 65c; 25 lbs., $1.50; 50 lbs., $2.50; 100 lbs., $4.00; 500 lbs., $17.50; 1000 lbs., $32.00; 1 ton, $60.00.

Nitrate of Lime (Equal to Nitrate of Soda)—5 lbs., 40c ; 25 lbs., $1.50; 100 lbs., $5.00.

Stim-U-Plant—Best concentrated fertilizer for house plants and small plots. Price, 25 tablets, 25c; 100 tablets, 75c; 1000 tablets (in pail), $3.50.

Vigoro—Best general purpose fertilizer for Shrubbery, Vines, Lawns, Gardens, etc. Circular free. Prices, 5 lbs., 40c; 25 lbs., $1.50; 50 lbs., $2.75; 100 lbs., $5.00.

INSECTICIDES AND FUNGICIDES

Black Leaf 40—For plant lice, thrip and red spider. 1 oz., 35c; ½ lb., $1.25; 2 lbs., $3.50.

Scalecide—1 qt., 75c; 1 gal., $1.75; 5 gals., $6.30; 10 gals., $11.50.

Slug Shot—For cabbage and currant worms. 1 lb., 20c; 5 lbs., 60c; 25 lbs., $2.75.

Antrol—For ants. 9 small jars and syrup. $2.00.

Snarol—For cutworms, grasshoppers, snails, slugs and sowbugs. 1 lb., 50c; 3 lbs., $1.00; 15 lbs., $4.00.

Tobacco Dust—1 lb., 15c; 5 lbs., 50c; 25 lbs., $2.00.

Bordeaux Arsenate of Lead (Powder)—For fungous and leaf-eating insects. Can be used as a spray or dry for dusting. Fine for potatoes, celery, grapes, fruit trees, etc. 1 lb., 40c; 5 lbs., $1.75; 10 lbs., $3.00; 25 lbs., $6.00; 100 lbs., $20.00.

Lime Sulphur Compound (Powder)—1 lb., 40c; 5 lbs., $1.80; 10 lbs., $2.50; 25 lbs., $5.00; 50 lbs., $8.50; 100 lbs., $15.00.

Lime Sulphur Solution—1 qt., 60c; 1 gal., $1.10; 5 gals., $4.50; 10 gals., $7.00; 50 gals., $15.00.

MULCH PAPER

Type A—Rolls, 18 inches wide, 300 lineal yards to roll (27 lbs.), $3.00 per roll. 36 inches wide, 300 lineal yards to roll (53 lbs.), $6.00 per roll.

Type B—Rolls, 18 inches wide, 150 lineal yards to roll (30 lbs.), $3.00 per roll. 36 inches wide, 150 lineal yards to roll (60 lbs.), $6.00 per roll.

; These Astounding Bargain Offers!

> give us a trial order, we make the following unheard-of offers, just to get
ll that we will hold your trade in years to come. Just compare these prices
you to send us an order. We cannot afford to send more than one collec-
ind, at these prices, orders must amount to $1.00 or more. If you will agree
on receipt of the goods, we will forward postpaid, thereby saving the ex-
rges.

hampion strawber-

'armer raspberries,

mbian raspberries,

dewberry, $2.00.

ra, Lucile, Moore's

:s old, 3-5 ft., our
$2.50.

ear, cherry, peach,

inches in diameter.
arly Rose, Cobbler,

artha Washington,

years old, 50c.

2 years old, our

15 inches, 3 times

:ars, red, pink and

a Van Houtte), 2

3-year seedlings, 9-

12 inches, $1.00.
rdy climber, 35c.
roots, $1.00.
d Paniculata Cle-

ic; 25 Mixed Glad-

21. 10 German Iris, our selection varieties,
$1.00.

22. 12 blue Japanese Iris, medium, $1.00.

23. 1 each, six colors (six varieties), best
Dahlias, medium size tubers, $1.00. 25 Dahlias,
mixed colors, $1.00.

24. Hardy Phlox, 1 each, Europa, F. G. Von
Lassburg and Michael Buchner, 50c; 4 of each,
$1.50.

25. 10 Hollyhocks, assorted colors, medium
plants, $1.00.

26. 15 Sweet William, assorted colors, medium plants, $1.00.

27. 10 Golden Glow plants, $1.50.

28. 6 Rhubarb roots (Linneaus), 1 year, 50c;
15 for $1.00.

29. 100 quarts or pint berry baskets, $1.00.

30. 4 pink Peonies, assorted kinds, $1.00.

31. 15 S. C., R. I. Red, Hatching Eggs, $1.00;
30, $1.75; 100, $5.00.

32. Geraniums, 20 kinds, 15c each; $1.25 per
10; $8.00 per 100.

33. 7 Cinnamon Vine tubers, 50c; 15 for
$1.00.

34. 12 Variegated Vinca, $1.00; 100, $8.00.

35. Hybridized potato seeds, 10c per packet;
10 packets, 75c.

36. Everbearing strawberry seeds, assorted
kinds, packet, 25c; 5 packets, $1.00.

37. Golden Bantam Seed Corn, packet, 10c;
pint, 30c; 1 quart, 50c.

38. 1 Oswego Apple tree, 3-5 ft., 50c.

39. 50 Everbearing strawberry plants, 2 varieties, $1.50.

Landscape Service

the benefit of our experience to patrons in planning new grounds or re-
le, we do not advise our customers to attempt any extensive planting of choice
onsulting an authority on the subject. During the late summer and fall
is available for consultation and supervision of landscape developments any-
ice from Pulaski. Our rates are reasonable, but we do not offer the so-called
. used to promote the sale of ornamentals.

or a
r list
imes

COPY OF CERTIFICATE OF INSPECTION No. 380
STATE OF NEW YORK
DEPARTMENT OF FARMS AND MARKETS

Four Choice Fruits for the Garden

PREMIER STRAWBERRY
Most popular early market
strawberry. 10 plants 50c; 25,
75c; 100, $1.50; 1000, $10.00.

COLUMBIAN RASPBERRY
Succeeds over a wider range than any other raspberry.
The farmer and home owner's raspberry. 10 plants 75c;
25, $1.25; 100, $4.00.

CACO GRAPE
Delicious, hardy, vigorous. 75c each; $7.00
per 10.

PLUM FARMER RASPBERRY
Most popular of all blackcap raspberries. Early, sweet,
rich, prolific, hardy, unsurpassed. 10 plants 60c;
25, $1.00; 100, $3.00; 1000, $25.00.

CPSIA information can be obtained
at www.ICGtesting.com
Printed in the USA
BVHW031221021118
531991BV00008B/712/P

9 780365 057550